KNOWN

embracing Whose you are in a social media world

SHELBEY KENDALL

To the women out there struggling with feeling alone in such a connected world.

This is for you.

CONTENTS

AUTHOR'S NOTE

As of February 2019, 95 million new photos are posted on Instagram per day. There are over 2 billion people of the world's population on Facebook and 5 new profiles are created per second. 74% of American Facebook users visit daily, with half of those checking in multiple times a day.

This frequency of social media usage is important for us to recognize, because it allows us to see how social media has become a massive part of our society today.

I always knew I wanted to become an author. I would create small handmade booklets for my parents to purchase as a child. In Junior High, I wrote "write a book" on my dream board. I've started and stopped several different book ideas.

God beautifully prepared me to mesh my social media struggles with my desire for writing and here we are—a book in your hands.

Throughout this book, I use a lot of Kingdom language. I wanted to explain before you dove in deep.

Take delight in the Lord, and he will give you your heart's desires.

Psalms 37:4

This verse is many times misused in our society when it comes to worldly success, motives, and gain. The truth is when we delight in the Lord and His Ways (the Kingdom way), He will give us the desires of our hearts because our desires will become in alignment with His.

He does not bend His ways to our ways in order to please us. We learn to turn away from the ways of this world in order to ask what is pleasing to Him. We learn to lean into Him and fully trust Him with the life He has so graciously given us.

We recognize that our Father, Who created us intentionally and with purpose, has desires for us beyond our own worldly understanding.

When we choose to be part of His Kingdom, we choose to put away our own selfish desires for status in this world. This is such an integral part of learning to embracing Whose you are in this social media world.

Whose we are in Him is so much greater than who we are in this world.

Before we explore this more in depth through the book, I have a few people to thank for their incredible support.

My amazing husband is the most supportive individual on this planet I know. From Facebook to marriage vows in about 6 months, our marriage is proof good can come from social media. He not only gives me grace when I've had to prioritize writing over many other things in our house, but he has encouraged it. He does the dishes. He lets me sleep. He brings me coffee. I am so thankful for his deep encouragement.

I have this tribe of friends that are always in my corner. They've been there when I've struggled through rejection of others and reminded me of the ways I was created beautifully and intentionally. I know they'd fight for me. I didn't have the best experience with relationships with girls growing up. These women have redeemed my idea of how friendships with women can be. They are all fierce in their own ways and I am so incredibly proud to call them my friends. You all know who you are!

My parents. I could write a book just on all the ways they've supported me in my short 29 years. They always gave me room for dreams, for experience, for growth, for hurt, and for figuring out life on my own. They never boxed me in. They always allowed me the opportunity to soar. For that, I am grateful. I love you both so much!

And then there's you! Thank you for picking up this book! Thank you for supporting the vision God gave me for my life. I hope that there is something within the words in this book that touches you, that convicts you, that encourages you, that allows you to feel how deeply loved you truly are. I am excited for you!

I am incredibly grateful to be a vessel for God's work. Praise Him for seeing my worth and allowing me to drop my insecurities the world labels me with so I can fully step into Whose I am in Him. Glory to God!

-1-

THIS IS FOR YOU

Hey friend.

These pages are full of words that were written for you. For the woman struggling with feeling seen and known and loved. For the woman who wants to believe they are more than what they are right now, but also enough in who they are currently. For the woman who knows they were called to be more and do more for the Kingdom of God. For the woman who struggles with pressure the world places upon her to be seen in the realm of social media. For the woman who struggles allowing her story to be heard, because it may be attacked for validity or with the intention to shame.

God gently shook me as He told me to pour out these words that are now here in this book for you to read, knowing women of today need to hear them.

You see, I have struggled.

Social media in the society we live in today has caused me to welcome unnecessary lies to warp my view of who I am.

When uncovering these lies, I also uncovered that I am far from being alone.

Due to the constant updates to keep up with our social media posts, many have suffered from a warped viewpoint of themselves.

I believe that we have an embedded desire within us that craves the feeling of being known. Of being known for the deepest parts of us that make up who we are. Of being known in a way that allows us to feel free in the person we were created to be. Of being known in a way that sheds the brokenness like a locust sheds its' skin, leaving it behind to dissolve into dust so its' true colors sparkle and are seen in the gleaming light.

We want to sparkle.

We want to be seen.

We want to live life for something bigger than ourselves.

We want to be known.

In a sea of millions of faces, we want to feel set apart. In a sky of a million stars, we want to shine brighter. We want to radiate from the crowd. Maybe not in a blatantly obvious way, but in a way that people would say recognize us and do so with a smile and a deep respect for who we are.

I've thirsted for this feeling so intensely that I have allowed it to consume me and become one of the focus points of my life. The dangerous part with allowing something to consume you is that if it isn't something healthy to be immersed into, it can create damage within ourselves and to the ones around us.

Being consumed by something is an entire body and mind experience. When our mind is not satisfied with what is happening in our life, we can feel it throughout our body. Another word for consume is devour. I have been devoured by the desire to be known.

The most unfortunate part about this is within the fact that many times when we are seeking something to make us feel freer in our life, we leave out that true freedom rests in Jesus Christ. So, in not seeking Him first, we chase a never-ending path that will continue to weave in and out of fear, insecurities, selfishness and small mountains of victory followed by deep pits of sitting in failure or regret that allow us to feel never enough.

We choose a path that is treacherous when we forget to seek Him first, even if it was inadvertent.

Social media has created a community arena that allows us to connect with other people. It can be an incredible resource to us, but it can also be a detour to stepping onto that never-ending path to seek validation and approval from other people instead of seeking validation from God.

Friend, I see you.

My feet get tripped up and I find myself stumbling down the path of world validation where I've taken wrong turns running into fear, insecurities and the belief that I am enough within myself or I'm not enough at all. I arrive at the idea that I don't need help. The idea that I can make myself known by others within my own power and that once they really see me, they'd accept me and love me.

As I write this book, it drips in unfortunate experience. I say unfortunate because in order to come to you in a place of realness and vulnerability, I had to wrestle with my own quest for being known by the world. I had to wade in deeper and immerse myself in my own pain to feel like the words I write are coated in love and understanding for you, but also in pressing boldness that would create a desire within you to act and break free of any chains that Satan has bound you in.

You are known deeply by a God who sees all of you and He has a crazy amount of freedom planned for you. In order to receive it, you must surrender your fear and obsession with molding yourself into the person you want other people to see, so they like you. You must stop being preoccupied by the idea of being known by the world.

As I was going about some household chores in my home thinking about content for this book, God said quietly to me in a strong voice…

You were made for such a time as this.

If you keep silent at this time, relief and deliverance will come to the Jewish people from another place, but you and your father's family will be destroyed. Who knows, perhaps you have come to your position for such a time as this. Esther 4:14

Esther became royalty during a time where she was needed to provide deliverance for her people, but it depended on her choice to not remain quiet. She had to speak up. She was placed in a position that allowed her to use her voice in a way that could be incredibly powerful.

She didn't choose that position initially. Esther did not want to go through the process that was required in order to come to the king to either be accepted or rejected. She didn't care about titles.

Esther became queen and the time came for her to choose whether she would shy away from the opportunity to deliver her people or if she would use that chance and speak up.

God would have saved her people with or without her. God's work will be done, but we have the amazing opportunity to be part of His work.

We are given choice.

Esther spoke up.

In the end, she helped save lives because she surrendered herself to the opportunity that was presented in front of her. She changed the world.

She did not happen upon that position by chance.

She was put there for that specific time and for that specific opportunity.

I don't believe that Esther operated under the desire to be known by other people. She did not long for the acceptance of the world, and she didn't work to attain that position for others to admire her.

She was first deeply known by a loving Father who saw her strengths and her ability. He knew her for who He created within her.

Because she was not blinded by the desire to be known by the world, she was able to open her eyes wide to what her heavenly Father needed from her.

We unintentionally blind ourselves when we focus on the what the world wishes from us which causes us to miss how we can be used for His good.

We live in a different world today than Esther's world, but I believe that we are here because we were all created for such a time as this.

God provides us with opportunity to show up in the "right now" to provide deliverance to His people. We must choose to speak up. We must choose to stand out for Him and not for ourselves. We are not here on accident.

You, dear friend, were created for the right now.

You did not happen because of chance; you were created on purpose for a purpose.

Our world today consists of countless measures of social media connection unlike the days of Esther.

Social media presents itself as an opportunity for us to change the world. It gives us a chance to make an impact. However, it also creates more issues that must be dealt with that can cause us to pause and be distracted from our true purpose.

The past few years I've been tracking my social media usage and the emotions that I attach to it.

We are constantly scrolling everyone else's highlight reels aimlessly. Normally, we just scroll to scroll. We have never been so connected and so disconnected at one time.

We scroll by giving out "likes" or "loves" or commenting, or not giving out anything at all.

We scroll by selfies, people's successes, vacation photos, Pinterest worthy interior design photos of friend's homes, adorable pregnant bump photos everyone is fangirling over, matching outfits on adorable kids and on and on and on.

Highlights.

In your face, all day long.

And although, we may look around and compare their highlight reels to our current circumstances, the trend I am seeing has nothing to do with how much better someone's life seems in the moment.

Sure, we can make ourselves feel left out and less than just from the sheer presence of someone's amazing photo, but I've realized that I immediately click on who has reacted on other posts and compare it to mine.

It is instantaneous. I barely even look at the photos anymore. I look directly at the people who are choosing to "like" or comment on them.

Those interactions.

The interactions that caused their posts to feel "more popular" than mine. The likes, the loves, the laughing faces, the comments.

I would look at all of that and then compare those interactions to the amount and types of interactions I was getting on my own content.

Why did that bother me so much?

Because the interactions meant people were engaged with their content. It meant people loved them and wanted to interact with them. Then, when I would have a post that I felt was amazing fall completely flat, it would make me feel "less than".

It wasn't about the vacations, the success, the perfect selfies…it was about being seen, being liked, and above all being known.

Interaction in my mind equated to being known.

I realized this deep need for being known kept me chasing perfect social media posts trying to gain more interaction, more love, more people. In fact, I would obsess trying to figure out how I could get my content more seen so that I could be more known among the people on my social media accounts.

I invested too much time and too many emotions in attempting for my content to be seen by others.

Then one day, I crumbled. Because my obsession was not fulfilling.

You see, I believe we serve a Higher Power and, in the attempt to control the process of being known by people, I had hindered my faith in giving it up to Him for His glory to be seen.

The fact that I had become prideful and ached for people knowing me more than knowing Him and being known by Him, was hard for me to swallow.

All because I wanted people to show up on my social media feed and want to know me.

Does this sound like you?

Are you desiring other people to show up to your newsfeed and accept you?

Are you ready to let go of that obsession? Of that comparison? Of that control?

When it comes to social media, there are unlimited reactions. There is no pie and only so many pieces. You are just as loved, welcomed, seen, heard, accepted, appreciated, and known as anyone else if you choose to decide that— because you friend, are a child of God.

You are loved uniquely.

You are set apart.

You are more precious than rubies.

You are known.

2 likes or 2,000.

0 comments or 100.

15 friends are 15,000.

You are known because of Whose you are sweet friend.

Let your joy bubble up. Let it take over your life. Don't allow the technicalities of social media to take over, to control you.

When we leave this world, we will not be judged by the success of our social media pages.

We will be known by a Savior who sees our heart and that heart reaction is worth millions.

-2-

UNPACKING THE PAST

When I began exploring the past years of my life, I realized I had given those years power to dictate how I perceived validation. Even though I had forgiven certain people in my past, I hadn't released the fear, shame, or control they had over me.

Because I was rejected...

Because I wasn't always valued...

Because of the brokenness I felt in feeling alone...

I allowed myself to perceive validation in the form of being liked by other people. I searched for people to accept my friend requests and follow me. I searched for people to react to my content. I searched to be raised to a status to be known by other people.

When people didn't accept me on social media, didn't react to my content, or didn't see my value, it would hurt me more deeply than it should have.

You can't press forward towards freedom when your heart is held captive by the past.

Past people, experiences, and events have shaped you into the person you are today, but they do not get to define who you are.

You can continually allow your past to creep into your present. You can end up searching for approval from other people to make you feel better about yourself. You can still be fighting demons from your past that are keeping you from making progress forward.

Does any of this sound like you?

You may have different details of your story, but are you allowing something from your past to keep you in bondage from being able to move forward freely?

The world is full of ways to keep us in bondage to keep us from taking steps forward in our walk with Christ.

"Do not remember the past events, pay no attention to things of old. Look, I am about to do something new; even now it is coming. Do you not see it?" Isaiah 43:18-19

For so long I could not see the new that was coming because I was held in bondage from my past.

We are told to put our past behind us. We need to break out of the shackles we've allowed our past to keep us in, so we can push forward in new freedom.

To do this we have to identify past moments, people, words, or actions that caused us to be fearful, because that same fear can be controlling our actions and thoughts today.

Since we are dealing with social media and a desire to be known by the world, we need to be able to identify situations in our past that may have triggered that desire.

What has caused you to seek out the validation of others to be known by the world?

Let's unpack part of my story.

I've allowed shame and fear from my past to keep me silent, even when pain sharply vibrated within me.

I've been silenced by others when I finally allowed words to accompany my pain. They didn't see my feelings as valid.

I've been judged for things I've done or said out of my attempt to find freedom beyond survival. I allowed that judgment to rob me of finding joy.

I've been fearful of how my story may look to others and if it will bring on worldly attack.

The truth is, the shame and fear that was once attached to me, kept me from being able to move forward in the ways God desired for me. It allowed me to search for acceptance on social media. I longed for "likes" to feel loved, for follows to feel desired, and for status to feel worthy.

I sought after worldly praise to try to rebuild myself when I felt torn down.

The story I journeyed out was difficult to walk through during a long season of my life. Part of the difficulty was due to my young age, but it was mostly due to my inexperience with how Satan operates to silence God's people before they can become strong enough to own God's truth.

I've always been a Christian. My car tag during my teen years was personalized to say GODSGRL. I was considered the "Christian girl" or the "goody-two shoes" in a small rural school.

Even though I had the outwardly labels, the confidence in Whose I was, was absent.

I had no desire to do anything that was rebellious. I didn't want to attend parties. I wanted to abstain from doing anything that was outside of parental or school authority. I simply wanted to be the nice girl.

With all that being said, I was not perfect. However, I felt the judgment from others who believed I was. I had a target slapped on my back.

It began small enough. Girls would make some snide comment covering it in giggles so others would think it was a joke. As months went by, it began to grow. The small verbal and emotional attacks didn't feel so small anymore.

The rejection from my female peers was difficult, but the attacks from them were suffocating.

I would go home from school, lay in my bed, and cry.

Living in a small town meant you never escaped the same group of people. Small towns are usually seen as places of safety, but I only felt trapped.

I remember walking out on my favorite sport.

I remember receiving an e-mail that detailed everything wrong about me.

I remember avoiding the girl's locker room to avoid confrontation or mockery.

I remember being invited to a party, but being the only girl not invited to the sleepover afterward.

I remember hearing about how girls were going to attempt to steal my boyfriend.

I remember using a relationship as my shelter, even when the relationship wasn't good for either person.

I remember the fleeting moments I would consider taking my own life.

I never wanted to retaliate, but I wanted to be freed.

I eventually began to drown in my own hurt, because I didn't take a stand for myself. Even though I would continually slap a smile on my face to hide the pain, it was simply a band-aid for the swirling emotions and words that were slowing drowning me from within.

Words hold power.

Death and life are in the power of the tongue, and those who love it will love its fruit. Proverbs 18:21

I had allowed their words to penetrate my exterior and wreak havoc within me as it pleased. What comes up against us can eventually become a part of our identity if we don't separate ourselves from it.

I constantly asked, "Why me?"

I had created this victim mentality that kept me from allowing victory in my life.

We can get so wrapped up in how we've been wronged that we allow it to become part of who we are and then, we struggle with how to heal ourselves of it.

One man was there who had been disabled for thirty-eight years. When Jesus saw him lying there and realized he had already been there a long time, he said to him, "Do you want to get well?" John 5:5-6

He didn't ask for the man's story. Jesus wasn't going to restrict healing him due to details. He simply wanted to know if the man wanted to be healed. He called the man out who had been laying there a victim to his disease for years.

Are you carrying a story within you that is keeping you from true redemption?

Do you have unhealed pain from your past that you have held yourself victim to?

God offers us wholeness in Him.

We cannot walk forward in the freedom from our hurts when we won't ask for the healing.

So many times, we will choose to bury hurt instead of allowing it to surface and actually deal with it. I always defaulted to bury hurt since it was a quick, temporary fix.

A few years ago, some of that hurt I had buried resurfaced.

God has continuously told me to own my story and use it for His good.

I've rejected His request many times, because I knew it would allow me to look vulnerable to attack.

However, when this hurt resurfaced, I decided to attempt to use it. I wrote a blog post revealing some hurts of my past. I didn't go too deep into details and I mentioned no names. I was simply trying to explore this new idea of utilizing pieces of my story to help others feel like they were not alone if they'd experienced a similar past.

The blog post was shared by one of the girls who had hurt me.

I remember getting a screenshot of the shared post from one of my friends along with many comments from others tearing me apart.

I remember one remark detailing how there was no way I was so hurt, because I was football homecoming queen. I guess this makes me living proof that a title can't produce freedom.

These are the types of comments and action that makes social media viewed as a place of destruction.

I was beginning to sink under the pain of their words once again, and then it happened. A couple girls who had once hurt me began defending me.

Those past hurts that resurfaced with the fresh attack on social media felt validated by past offenders. Women who had recognized the hurt that was caused, called it out.

It was a fleeting moment of worldly validation. I was grateful for it. It felt good to feel seen for how I had once felt. I was grateful for their brave honesty and their desire to stand up for me.

Worldly validation is fleeting, just like that homecoming title and tiara. Even though I was defended, I still allowed the attack to penetrate my exterior.

I didn't write for an entire year.

I had a difficult time trying to use any part of my story and allowing it to be seen because of what had happened. I had tried being vulnerable and transparent and it ended with me being more hurt and more fearful.

I feared another attack.

An attack from one person.

I was allowing myself to remain a victim because of the fear I had from someone who had once made me feel so little about myself.

It is so easy to shrink back when you are attacked. It is so easy to remain a victim to your past when you don't release all your hurt and shame.

On a Sunday morning drive to church, I confessed to my husband the fears I had about releasing pieces of my past in this chapter to the world. I was fearful that others who knew me from my past would not validate my personal emotions and battles I had experienced.

What if others saw my situation differently?

I didn't get to listen to the church message that Sunday as I was busy wrestling our three-year-old, but my husband re-shared it with me on our way back home.

Joseph and the amazing, colored coat.

Now Israel loved Joseph more than his other sons because Joseph was a son born to him in his old age, and he made a robe of many colors for him. When his brothers saw that their father loved him more than all his brothers, they hated him and could not bring themselves to speak peaceably to him. Genesis 37:3-4

This love that his father had for him was just the beginning. Joseph also began having dreams where his brothers and parents were bowing down to him and he openly shared about these dreams.

Jealously was brewing. His brothers hated Joseph. Despised him. They wanted him gone.

So, they got rid of him. Then, they denied the truth about what happened to him for years.

What does Joseph do when it all comes full circle and they are begging him for rations of grain, so they do not die of starvation during a time of famine?

He forgives them.

He even goes to say that what they did, even though it was out of ill intent, was **used for good**.

Joseph did not wrap his identity around a victim mentality.

God takes what is bad and broken in our lives and He creates goodness out of it.

Joseph believed God had sent him before his family to save them.

If horrible things happened to you, know that you have the freedom to release it. Ill intentions against you do not get to break you and keep you broken. Your past does not get to own you and keep you from moving forward. Your past may be part of your story, but it is not your entire story.

Allow the One who created you to validate your worth. You do not need validation from the world or by the people who created the hurt in the first place.

There is no story Jesus cannot redeem. Jesus simply asks you if you want to be healed from your disease.

He wants you to see the newness in front of you.

I sat in my room one day and had this gripping feeling around my heart that was keeping me from moving forward to find the new things set out for me, by Him. I fell to my knees and asked God to tell me what was pausing my footsteps forward. Shame suddenly washed over me. I thought I had let go of the hurt of my past, but the shame was still present.

I should have stood up for myself.

I should have been able to say "no".

I should have been able to take better care of myself before I had thoughts that spiraled me into depression.

The list of "should have's" began piling high.

I was still carrying around an unbelief from my past story. An unbelief that was keeping me captive. I had wanted the healing earlier, but I hadn't fully given myself over.

We keep ourselves from the healing when we don't believe we are worthy of it. A healed life is a new life and sometimes, we don't believe we deserve it.

The skeptic within me looks back and wonders how anyone could truly wipe my slate clean. The skeptic within me hinders my faith in His grace.

Jesus held His arms out and welcomed in the death that was mine.

Jesus broke my chains that kept me in bondage to my iniquities.

If I could shed my unbelief, how would I walk out this new life? What do those steps look like?

When you finally break off the parts of you that are keeping you in bondage, you lose part of you that you have known.

We want freedom, right?

Or are we like the man who laid beside the stream for thirty-eight years, fearful of the new life he'd have to learn how to journey out?

After this, Jesus found him in the temple and said to him, "See, you are well. Do not sin anymore, so that something worse doesn't happen to you." John 5:14

We aren't just asking for a healing from our past. We are asking for Jesus to make us whole. We are asking for new life. Jesus instructed the man after being healed to refrain from sin so that he is kept well.

Whole living means being cautious about the sin that arises in your life and being responsible for it.

Are we scared to let go of the things from our past because walking forward in freedom means a deeper responsibility of walking like Jesus?

Taking on that kind of responsibility is giving up our excuses.

Well… I crave acceptance from other people, because I was constantly rejected.

Well… I have a hard time loving other people, because I was told I was unlovable.

Well… I throw up walls when it comes to relationships, because I'm scared of letting anyone in again.

Well… I attack others, because I'm scared of being vulnerable and letting others see my shortcomings.

When you choose new living, you are choosing to guard yourself from old patterns that are sinful.

Take off your former way of life, the old self that is corrupted by deceitful desires, to be renewed in the spirit of your minds, and to put on the new self, the one created according to God's likeness in righteousness and purity of the truth. Ephesians 4:22-24

You cannot move forward in God's freedom until you have removed yourself from your past self.

You can't wear old pants and a new shirt.

You must strip yourself of the bondage the world has you in from your past, so you can fully press into the fullness of who you are in God.

You do not have to sit in unbelief.

You do not need excuses to fall back on when you fail.

Choose Christ's victory over your victim story. Allow your story to be used to build His Kingdom, not to keep you from it. You are not who you once were, you are who you are becoming.

It's your turn to dig deep. Allow the hurts in your past experiences and relationships you've had to resurface. Sort through them and figure out why you may search for acceptance, flattery or status on social media. Identify where you need healing and then choose to receive it.

Don't allow the things you have known in your life to keep you in bondage from the growth you desire.

Faith and fear both require you to believe in something you cannot see.
You choose. - Bob Proctor

We get to **choose**.

Will you choose fear that keeps you from the good life God desires for you or will you choose faith that allows you to move forward knowing He has taken every footstep before you?

Don't allow the insecurities of your past self to rule over your present or future self.

Fear smiles smugly knowing he can keep us in captivity with our past thoughts and feelings. I say smile smugly back at fear letting him know that your God is bigger and will use those past thoughts and feelings for His greater good.

Make fear tremble instead of allowing fear to make your own knees buckle.

Surrender your past to the victory of God and choose the healing He is offering you.

Your past needs unpacking. It's sat in its' luggage too long.

ACCEPTANCE IN CHRIST

The struggle with wanting to be known by the world is that it creates fear that you are not enough for the people who follow you, interact with you, or do life with you. Power is given to the people who give or withhold validation as they see fit.

We begin to base our worth on acceptance by people. We use our social media pages to present ourselves as someone they will accept. We don't fully show up in our vulnerability on social media or in real life interactions, fearing we may be too much for someone to "like".

Several years ago, I began curating the content of my social media page for it to be less offensive to others. I desired for others to like me. I poured out kindness with the intention of others accepting what they saw.

I knew that people judged on appearance. If I appeared to be someone who loved with words that always made others feel good, then surely, I would be a well-loved person.

Just as we have been approved by God to be entrusted with the gospel, so we speak, not to please people, but rather God, who examines our hearts. For we never used flattering speech, as you know, or had greedy motives—God is our witness—and we didn't seek glory from people, either from you or from others. 1 Thessalonians 2:4-5

Paul addressed the church of Thessalonians with an understanding that he and his friends spreading the Gospel would be met with opposition. They did not try to impress the people around them with their words in order to gain acceptance by the people they spoke to.

God knew their hearts and knew that self-glory was not a motive.

They spoke out of gentleness. They spoke with intention to encourage and comfort, but also to convict those to live in a way that is pleasing to God.

I may have been encouraging in my words and many times in my actions, but my people pleaser radar was strong. The motive of my heart was to flatter others and to create a persona of myself they would easily accept. I am known by many to give multiple gifts. Gift giving is my love language. I would purchase food or fun items for others several times a month and surprise people with it. Spreading kindness is not the issue, it's the motive behind. There were many times I gave with the intention of acceptance.

We can give everything away but when it is done with the wrong motive, it won't be fulfilling. I desired acceptance by the people around me more than acceptance by Christ.

The other day I noticed someone I had once showered with gifts and words had unfriended me on Facebook.

People will take all the flattery you pour out, but that doesn't mean they truly accept you. When you attach validation to the gifting, you welcome in the opportunity to be hurt by the rejection.

Just as we relinquished the power from the fear we had in insecurities from our past, we must also take the power back from the people we base our acceptance level on.

Social media deeply entangles itself in the process of acceptance. It's easy for us to become distracted by the ways of this world when we are constantly checking our screens.

I earned this amazing retreat not long ago. I had the opportunity to stay in a fancy hotel, travel to a new place I hadn't been and be showered with gifts. My husband went with me and although he fully enjoyed the trip, I'm sure he would have loved to avoid the breakdown that was about to happen within me.

I was all fancied up in an elegant dress I felt like I stole for the entire $14 it cost me. I did my hair, slipped into some heels that were so high I wanted to burn every stiletto my eyes gazed upon for months after and felt good about myself. It was the first night there and I was incredibly excited to begin the retreat in style.

There was a set up to take photos with perfect lighting. I was so excited to take a good photo with my husband while we were all fancied up. It only took one shot to get an amazing photo and I was excited to share it with my friends.

You should know a few things before the rest of the story goes on.

First, my normal consists of yoga pants and possibly a swipe of mascara every day. Getting to this celebrity stage of fancy, made this night a big deal and I was going to post everything on social media.

Secondly, this retreat was earned because of an accomplishment I had achieved within a company I build a business with. It is a naturally celebrated event and I was excited for my time to be in that spotlight.

I posted the photo on social media quickly and went about enjoying the entertainment and food for the evening. Later that night I checked my post to find many reactions on it, but there were a few names missing from that list I had expected to show up to celebrate my accomplishment.

You've been there right?

Waiting for the validation of someone else to confirm how amazing you are?

Waiting to see them heart up your photo and make some gushy comment about how amazing you look?

The next day went by and still nothing on that post from those select individuals.

I created other content throughout the event and posted away. Nothing on those either.

The entire retreat went by and I wrestled intensely with this issue of desiring their validation. Others on the retreat were getting showered in gifts and words of affirmation. I was so preoccupied from wondering where my accolades from others were, that I allowed myself to break down.

I felt left out, unappreciated, and less than.

But who was at fault here?

Could these people have made an effort to celebrate this accomplishment? Yes, but they didn't.

My initial reaction was one of anger. Many times, we become tunnel-focused. We believe the way we view something is the only right way.

All a person's ways seem right to him, but the Lord weighs the heart.
Proverbs 21:2

Social media amplifies our prideful ways because we can assert our idea of rightness with the quick touch on our screen.

After feeling hurt and allowing my pride to subside, shame flooded over me. I recognized that the blame for my emotions laid on my own shoulders. Shoulders that were sinking under the heaviness of shame, realizing that my desire for people's validation was a broken behavior I had created myself.

I was seeking validation from people instead of placing my validation within the One who sees me and knows me fully.

The one who conceals his sins will not prosper, but whoever confesses and renounces them will find mercy. Proverbs 28:13

I had to break myself of my sin through confession, knowing that in doing so I could begin to realign myself within the grace of God.

Giving people power to validate who you are will always be a treacherous road to stumble around on because they control how you feel about yourself.

Giving away power over your emotions to another person is a dangerous situation. It is like handing over the button to a detonator where if they decide to press it a self-destruct bomb goes off inside your heart. They control your emotions which in turn, can also control your actions and your words.

When they become disappointed in how you reacted in a situation, they press the button.

When they decide you said something that they felt offended by, they press the button.

When you do anything that doesn't align with what they believe, they press the button.

The detonator keeps going off within you and you become a reaction to a person's opinion of your life.

Friend, God gave you purpose before anyone else had an opinion. The problem is you have given the power of how you feel to someone else.

There isn't a single human that deserves to control another's emotions. We may find those who want the best for us, but humans continually disappoint one another when they are the sole source of our emotional security.

This puts too much pressure on our relationships. Relationships that could be life-building can turn destructive, because we allow someone else to validate our life choices.

I once placed all my emotional security in one relationship. It was constantly disappointing. One moment I would be soaring high on validation and the next I would be buried under deep hurt and shame.

People were not created to possess the power to control someone else's emotions.

It's a cycle of disappointment and self-destruction.

We have the control to give up and surrender this cycle.

We don't have to be disappointed by other people constantly and we don't have to be a disappointment to other people, because we can take away the detonator. We don't need to be accepted by the world, instead we need to learn how to accept ourselves as we are now and as the person we are growing into.

Self-acceptance is a critical part in letting go of the need for being known by the world.

Notice I said self-acceptance. This is different from self-love.

We live in a world where self-love is heavily promoted. Quotes on loving yourself often pop up in my newsfeed.

To fall in love with yourself is the first secret to happiness.

The relationship with yourself sets the tone for every other relationship you have.

You alone are enough. You have nothing to prove to anyone.

Loving yourself isn't vanity. It is sanity.

Self-love is an ocean and your heart is a vessel. Make it full, and any excess will spill over into the lives of other people you hold dear. But you must come first.

Now these quotes sound good, don't they?

I think I've even used a couple of these quotes or similar ones in my past because we live in a self-love society and I have fallen victim to it. We are constantly told that we are enough within ourselves and we don't need anyone else to confirm that.

Although it is true that we don't need the world or anyone of the world to validate us, we also must realize that we aren't enough by ourselves.

It isn't you that makes you enough.

It isn't your success, your abilities, your thoughts, your kindness, your attitude, your "you"ness that makes you enough.

For it is not the one commending himself who is approved, but the one the Lord commends. 2 Corinthians 10:18

There is this blurred line we have created in our self-empowering, self-loving culture.

We have bought into the belief that if we strip away the broken parts of us, shake off the judgment of other people, and charge ahead in full pursuit of what will make us happy, we have a "right" to that.

When we decide to rid ourselves of being accepted by people, we tend to go to the complete opposite side of the spectrum. We forge ahead with the idea that we have this unsaid permission to do what we want to do, to say what we want to say, and to achieve the things we want to achieve. We can do it all by ourselves because of ourselves.

I picture a stubborn toddler who is constantly telling their parent "all by myself" when asked if he or she needs help. Even when you can clearly tell there are going to be moments help will be needed.

We are those selfish toddlers.

We have decided that the world can sit back and watch. We don't need any help to achieve the things we want to achieve in our life or be the person we want to become.

Instead of seeking the approval of the world, we are now charging ahead to spite the world.

"Just watch me."

Take that world. I got this on my own. Watch me succeed.

The biggest revenge is massive success. — Frank Sinatra

Revenge is a tactic that revolves around self. It screams insecurities even when it appears to be confidence.

Friend, when this happens people are still living for the world. They may not be living for approval, but they want to prove the world wrong. Therefore, the focus is still on the world and its' worldly ways.

As with toddlers, something tends to happen that makes the toddler realize that help is sometimes required. They learn the lesson of humbleness.

Being humble means having no excess of pride. The above scenario of telling the world off, is an act of pride.

We can easily swing the pendulum from shame to pride when we dive into the world of self-love.

Living for yourself is living for the world.

We are given messages attempting to encourage us that if we try hard enough, we can have anything we desire to achieve. We are given messages filling us with these huge dreams that give us permission to sacrifice callings that have been placed in our life in order to chase happiness. We can end up sacrificing our Kingdom callings for our own temples to be erected to receive praise in the pursuit of our own desires.

The world may as well have its' own quote.

Those who work hard enough for what they want are worthy of receiving it. -The World

This is a vicious cycle allowing thousands of people to hustle hard after the shiny splendors of the world and turn away from the grandeurs of God.

These are some synonyms of self-love: conceited, egotistic, self-centered, self-involved, stuck-up, vain.

Some may argue and say that you cannot love others without first working on loving yourself. Some say self-love is the opposite of being self-centered because it gives you a better ability to pour yourself out to others. We embrace this entire philosophy of putting on our oxygen mask before putting the mask onto the faces of others. However, the oxygen mask has evolved into an additional facial, massage, and shopping spree to "treat 'yo self!'".

We aren't talking about self-care (which any of the above can be with the correct attitude behind it); we are talking about an entire lifestyle of how you operate in your daily life.

He said to him, "Love the Lord your God with all your heart, with all your soul, and with all your mind. This is the greatest and most important command. The second is like it: Love your neighbor as yourself. All the Law and the Prophets depend on these two commands.
Matthew 22:37-40

Notice how the mention of loving oneself was not part of the most important commandments?

We cannot put ourselves first.

Loving ourselves does not create an overflow for others around us. Loving the Lord creates that overflow.

We must drop this rebellious nature to prove others wrong. Confidence doesn't come from a self-manifested behavior. Confidence comes from owning Whose you are in God.

Even when it is uncomfortable. Even when others are in opposition. Even when you get unfriended.

It doesn't matter how many titles we earn, how many trophies we win, or how many accolades we receive, it all falls short when measured up to the glory of God.

We can puff up ourselves with good sounding phrases all day long, but we will eventually deflate because the world doesn't provide what we were created for.

There is a difference between those who forge ahead a path in God's grace and those who forge ahead a path in a prideful attitude that wants to prove worthiness to other people in their life.

Friend, we must stop chasing dreams for all the wrong reasons. We must stop giving ourselves sole credit when we do succeed. We need to learn to humble ourselves so that we don't rush forward with the purpose to make an impact for our own gain, but instead with the promise that we serve a God who gives so much more than we can offer up on our own merit.

While I do believe that we should always feel we are enough and love ourselves, it isn't because of anything we have done, said, or are known for.

It is because of **Whose** we are.

We deeply need to accept the redemption of Christ and fully embrace it.

You aren't meant to serve yourself.

Love consists in this: not that we love God, but that he loved us and sent his Son to be the atoning sacrifice for our sins. 1 John 4:10

When we choose acceptance in Christ, we choose the love of God.

We don't need to learn to love ourselves when we know God through His love.

His love overcomes our insecurities.

His love washes away our desire for worldly approval.

Through the sacrifice of His Son, we are given freedom to accept ourselves because of His love.

We are not complete within ourselves.

You are not that awesome on your own.

I'm not that awesome on my own.

We are only made enough because of the redemption we have found in Jesus Christ.

God looks at me and He looks at you. He tells us to come as we are. He calls us worthy and loved because we are redeemed by the blood of Christ. Our freedom was acquired on that cross.

Your acceptance isn't because of self-love or that you yourself have proved yourself worthy.

It isn't because the world has looked at you and called you good.

God doesn't look at your Facebook likes or how many people follow you on social media to see your worthiness.

He steps in and calls you enough because you are His, not because you are enough on your own.

The problem with self-love is that when we begin to believe that we are enough within ourselves, we take up all the space leaving no room for Him to show up and be praised in our brokenness and in our victories.

He can make our brokenness look like greatness. We can't do that on our own.

We don't need to sell ourselves to others or to our own self. We need to see ourselves as He sees us.

He sees you. He knows you.

You are known because of Him. You are known fully by Him. You are given the opportunity to be known in Him.

You are not known because of your attributes, your good deeds, your likability, or your success.

You are also not known because of your sins, the times you have stumbled, the people who dislike you, or your own failures.

He looks inward and He sees you despite your sinful nature.

He loves you despite…that judgmental thing you said yesterday.

He accepts you despite…the loving thing you could have said yesterday but withheld.

He calls you worthy despite…the really, incredibly, broken, ugly things you have ever done or said.

We are a fallen people. We cannot forget that. We must remember that we do not deserve to be loved, accepted, seen, and known in the way that we are by God. When we can finally grasp how truly amazing the acceptance God extends to us is, we can see the massive amount of grace that is poured out on us that can only be poured out by God. We cannot pour out that kind of grace ourselves and the world cannot pour out that kind of grace either.

There is not a single person walking on this Earth that can give you what God can.

Humans do not possess that power.

We are called to be in the most intimate relationship with a Father who redeems us and who uses our weaknesses for His strength and His goodness. He uses our victories and multiplies their value in His glory.

We are broken clay pots. We have tried sealing our cracks and making us brand new. We have tried hiding the cracks, doing anything to not draw attention to them. We don't want people to see the brokenness.

God can use that brokenness for His good as His light seeps in and shines through it. He heals the broken parts through His warm, blinding light of love and grace.

Therefore, I will most gladly boast all the more about my weaknesses, so that Christ's power may rise in me. So I take pleasure in weaknesses, insults, hardships, and in difficulties, for the sake of Christ. For when I am weak, then I am strong. 2 Corinthians 12:9-10

Your brokenness can be used for His good.

You must walk the road of transparency and vulnerability.

The journey of being in the Light, is one that is not afraid of what will be seen.

Therefore, we need to learn to have acceptance of ourselves through Christ.

We do not carry the load of our sins.

> *This is the judgement: The light has come into the world, and people loved darkness rather than the light because their deeds were evil. For everyone who does evil hates the light and avoids it, so that his deeds may not be exposed. But anyone who lives by the truth comes to the light, so that his works may be shown to be accomplished by God. John 3:19-21*

Transparency in who we once were, does not have power to define us, because our redemption was accomplished through ultimate love in God. We do not have to shoulder any shame.

Shame for the parts of us that we do not want to be seen.

Shame for the brokenness we have allowed in our life.

Shame for the things we have done or the things we have said about other people or about ourselves.

Friend, I have carried shame for years unknowingly. I carried shame for things that had happened to me, for things I had allowed, for ways I had reacted or didn't react, for not saying "no", for fear of rejection, and for allowing myself to become so depressed I wanted to end my own life.

Shame holds you within captivity.

In carrying that shame, I allowed parts of me to be hidden from the world, but it also kept God's work in me from being seen.

It is time to surrender the parts of yourself that you keep shoving down within. It is time to pull them up to the surface, wrestle with them and ask God to break them off you. You need to allow Him to show you that He can take your ugly parts and make beauty from them in His grace.

It is a painful process, but it is a redeeming process. It is the process where you let go of whatever is within you that creates a desire to be known and accepted by people of this world. It is a process where you break off whatever is causing you to fear rejection of others. This is the process of accepting His freedom. Freedom to see yourself in a new light, His Light, and allow it to consume you and completely flood out the fear of what others may think of you.

It allows you to submit a post of rawness, or simplicity, or tenderness, or truth, or anything that is placed on your beautifully beating heart and not allow the popularity of it to control your emotions.

It allows you to say something that you feel has rocked your world and then be okay if it doesn't rock someone else's world.

You are giving up the world to gain His peace in your life.

51

We always carry the death of Jesus in our body, so that the life of Jesus may also be displayed in our body. For we who live are always being given over to death for Jesus's sake, so that Jesus's life may also be displayed in our mortal flesh. So then, death is at work in us, but life in you. 2 Corinthians 4:11-12

We are a redemption story and it isn't complete until the day we are welcomed into our eternal home.

We are going to be challenged often. Persecuted. Tempted. Hurt. Given over to death of ourselves repeatedly, so that we can choose to act as Jesus would.

Why would we choose the option for dying to ourselves?

Because in dying to ourselves and our selfish desires, we choose the redemption Jesus claimed for us on the cross. When we die to ourselves, we live for the life graciously given to us.

We will make the right decisions at times and we may also make the wrong decisions.

Over this past year, I haven't always displayed Jesus in my actions. I've held onto a lot of guilt for different things I said or felt out of reaction to someone else.

When I have felt attacked, I immediately want to play defense.

I live in a small town. I love the slow pace and the quietness. However, in a small town when hurt happens, you don't necessarily ever escape it. You see the same people over and over again. This can create some tension between those who have hurt and those who have hurt back in reaction.

One wrong doesn't justify another wrong.

Although I cannot change a person who seeks to hurt through gossip, slander, rejection, or whatever means they use, I can learn to control my knee-jerk reactions.

We must battle the flesh in order to glorify God. We must die to our sinful behaviors so that He may live within us. We can choose redemption daily and walk that story out in our life.

Acceptance in Christ is rejection of the world.

We must learn to surrender our failures to God so we can rid ourselves of the shame we have attached to it. We also must learn to surrender our success, our victories, and our hard-earned titles to Him so we can rid ourselves of the struggle of being known by the world.

To be known by the world is acting in vanity, acting of your flesh. To be known by Him and to allow yourself to accept who you are because of Whose you are, is acting of His grace. To give Him both your failures and your success, is giving Him the power to act in your life in big and small ways to intercede in the lives of others in a bigger way than you could ever do on your own.

Your success is His success.

Your victories are His victories.

When you attach your worth to the name of Christ, you can be used in the most intimate, beautiful way that allows Christ to be known through you and for you to feel deeply known in Christ.

Those who chase self-love and the acceptance of others are missing the big picture. Their focus isn't on whose they are and being known in Christ, but instead it is on who they have made of themselves and how many people have validated their life choices.

You only need one life validation.

God's.

You don't need the acceptance of other people. You need to learn to accept yourself as you are right now. You need to surrender your past, your present and your future. You need to let go of any guilt that may be holding you back from accepting His invitation of redemption.

You are enough, because of Him.

You are worthy, because of Him.

You are known, because of Him.

Once the rhythm of your beating heart matches the love and grace He has poured out on you, you will realize that a life of true peace in all circumstances exists. You will realize that being known by an intimate God who knows all parts of you and accepts you fully, frees you from the desire to be known by anyone else.

You are broken, but your brokenness is redeemed in the ocean of God's grace.

You are imperfect, but your imperfectness is made whole in the redemption of Jesus Christ.

You have failed, but God has used your failures to bring about His glory.

You have succeeded, and God has used those victories to bring splendor to His name.

Self-acceptance because of Whose you are is a beautiful thing friend.

Fully embrace it and watch as the world's influence shrivels, because being of the world no longer matters or holds status in your mind or heart.

Can you feel the freedom in that?

This is the freedom of not chasing the cheers of the world but instead chasing down the glory of God. You were created to chase Him down. You were created with the desire to be known by Him. He meets you where you are and doesn't require you to "be somebody" by the standards of this world. Your shame is washed away. Your glory is His glory.

Don't shrink back with the intentions of hiding from the world.

Don't stand out with the intentions of being applauded by the world.

Stand firm in who you are because of Whose you are. Plant yourself. Root yourself. Accept yourself for Whose you are in Him, not who you are in this world.

-4-

SOCIAL MEDIA

If you decided on this book and made it this far through, undoubtedly social media plays some sort of role in your life.

The world we live in is one where social media has intertwined itself.

Social media, at the core, is a tool that we have the opportunity to use. Too many times we use it like a sword against ourselves or on others, instead of a tool of connection.

I have played the comparison game many times with other women trying to figure out where I fall short because of social media. People are placed on virtual pedestals that raise them to a status worthy of their follower's applause.

As hard as it is to say, I would let the huge followings and comments on others' social media feeds make me feel like I wasn't enough. Some of my dearest friends felt like enemies to me because their content was more popular than mine.

They hadn't intentionally done anything to make me feel less than. I fell victim to comparison and allowed it to create major issues and cause incredible struggle for me, for a long time.

I would sit in discontentment because I was more obsessed with making myself more known for my own status and gain, than pressing into the One who knows me deeply. I wasn't giving Him power to use my life in the way He intended it to be used for His glory.

I don't like to admit to my past obsession with social media, but like any addiction, it is disruptive and all-consuming. I had a difficult time escaping it. I would constantly refresh my screen. I don't know exactly what I was hoping for, but I found out that refreshing your feed can't refresh your soul.

We can accomplish so much more in our lives if we are not busy spending our time consumed by refreshing our social media feeds. Time is something we are constantly complaining about not having enough of, and yet there we sit, wasting it, refreshing our screens as if it doesn't really matter that much at all.

Social media can become an addiction. An empty addiction that constantly impedes on focusing on our true purpose.

I once heard someone said, "I create social media. I don't consume it."

I would say who this came from but I'm not 100% sure who she was. It was from the bathroom stall of a conference I was attending and a conversation I had overheard, so we will just call her "Random Bathroom Lady".

At first, I felt Random Bathroom Lady's words were harsh and came from a place of pride and ego. I believe she thought herself better than others who consumed social media, including her own followers who were consuming her content. How dare she believe that she can create content to be consumed by others and not be active in consuming others' content?

Then I began really reflecting on what Random Bathroom Lady said, and I realized that she had an incredibly valid point. In this social media world, it is too easy to become consumed and addicted. She is most likely protecting her own heart and protecting her own purpose.

It's possible she understands that she needs to be present on social media to shine His light, but she also guards herself. If she begins to consume the content, she may falter and fall into the snares of fear that social media sets to control us.

When I was struggling, I knew that I needed to re-evaluate where I placed my worth and where I received love. I also needed to learn how to quit consuming content that consumed my life.

Guard your heart above all else, for it is the source of life.

Proverbs 4:23

The victory comes from recognizing when we've lost control and figuring out how to remedy our addiction. When I struggle, I turn to His Word immediately knowing I need to fill myself up with whatever He has planned for me. I love to open my Bible randomly and allow whatever is on the pages to surround me. I go in with an open mind to connect lessons to my current circumstances.

There was a particular time when I was struggling that when I opened up the Bible, I was hit hard.

I opened to the fruits of the Spirit. Seems good to reflect on, right? However, the verses before the fruits of the Spirit are filled with that of the sinful nature.

Now the works of the flesh are obvious: sexual immorality, moral impurity, promiscuity, idolatry, sorcery, hatred, strife, jealousy, outbursts of anger, selfish ambitions, dissensions, factions, envy, drunkenness, carousing, and anything similar. I am warning you about these things— as I warned you before—that those who practice such things will not inherit the kingdom of God.

But the fruit of the Spirit is love, joy, peace, patience, kindness, goodness, faithfulness, gentleness, and self-control. The law is not against such things. Now those who belong to Christ Jesus have crucified the flesh with its passions and desires. If we live by the Spirit, let us also keep in step with the Spirit. Let us not become conceited, provoking one another, envying one another.

Galatians 5:19-26

In my faltering with comparison I realized that it was not only a work of the flesh, but one that would keep me from inheriting the Kingdom of God. It is jealousy and envy bred out of comparison.

We think of sinful nature as acts that are huge and blatantly obvious, but all of those mentioned above are of the flesh and can be used to form different types of negative addictions that cause us to stumble in our walk in the Spirit. In this case, our social media addiction can be formed by hatred, strife (a bitter spirit), jealousy, outburst of anger (hello negative social media posts), selfish ambitions (becoming known by people for your own gain), dissensions (also known as conflict and the disruption of harmony, which we know is ALL over social media), factions (being part of a clique or group that is contentious or self-seeking), and envy.

These things are all actions that in practice will cause us to not receive the Kingdom of God because it works in opposition of the fruits of the Spirit.

This doesn't mean that we won't stumble at times in our lives. But we have to recognize when we are sinking into the ways of the world through social media issues, instead of embracing the fruits of the Spirit and changing the atmosphere and community of social media.

I want to be the good fruit.

Let's just be really blunt here, friend.

Rejection by people on earth pales in comparison to being rejected at the pearly gates. When we can't break free of the chains that the negative aspects of social media can place hold on us, we can't live a life that is worthy of stepping inside the place where holiness lives.

Breaking the addiction of social media is necessary and in doing so, we also realize that we are capable of not only becoming the good fruit but showing others how to become the good fruit too.

In order to do so, we must allow the Spirit of God to change us. To flow through us. To work within us to become not just the best version of ourselves, but the version of ourselves that God intended us to become. The fruit of the Spirit is not created out of our own efforts. It is created only by the Spirit.

What does this mean?

Repentance.

Allowing Him to redeem us. Allowing Him to bear our sinful nature so that we are rid of it, freeing us to be able to become people who only consume the good fruit.

Breaking our social media addiction comes from surrender of ourselves and of our own effort, to be replaced by Him and His effort.

Do you obsess over it too? Do you allow your obsession to steal the goodness, the dreams, the God-given vision for your own life?

Our obsessions with social media can rip the very life that was intended beautifully and intentionally for us by a Father who wants to give us so much more than what we can give on our own.

I believe that our obsession grew from a desire to feel like we belonged to something more than ourselves. We longed for the community that social media can provide. We were created with the deep need for relationships and in our current world, many relationships are created and/or sustained using social media.

The beautiful part about this is, at the beginning, our intentions were most likely focused on connection with others. So, let's talk about our relationships.

How many of our relationships are surface level?

I'm talking both social media and our face-to-face communities.

Do we dig deeper to know a person's heart, or do we only catch the things about them that are obvious?

Most of the time we go through the motions of building relationships based on the things we see with our eyes instead of digging deep with intention. We make quick judgments. We create labels. We create distance from those that don't fit in with us and align with our beliefs or lifestyle. We cozy up to those that make us feel better about ourselves and how we live our lives.

One thing I know about people is they don't like to intentionally step into the uncomfortable.

Let's get a little personal.

How many times have you rolled your eyes, made a comment about someone, or unfriended somebody because they made you uncomfortable?

I'm not talking in a sleezy way of being uncomfortable. Unfriend the sleezy, please. I'm talking about the uncomfortable of intimidation. I'm talking about the uncomfortable of refusing to grow a relationship because of something that is important to the other person. I'm talking about the uncomfortable of recognizing that you may be judgmental.

We push away what could be Kingdom building friendships because of the uncomfortable.

Listen, I get it.

I completely understand that your ideals may not 100% align with someone else's. But are they supposed to?

Are we not constantly telling ourselves and others to embrace the person God has created them to be?

And yet, here we are, blatantly telling others through our rejections of one another, the complete opposite.

How are we supposed to rise up as a people for His Kingdom when we decide to tear the Kingdom apart before it can even stand up?

We are doing Satan's work for him. The devil should need to work a lot harder to keep the people of God from coming together and constructing plans to glorify God's mighty name.

Friend, the war we are preparing for is beyond surface level.

Surface level disagreement.

Surface level discomfort.

Surface level living.

"Flee from youthful passions, and pursue righteousness, faith, love and peace, along with those who call on the Lord from a pure heart. But

reject foolish and ignorant disputes, because you know that they breed quarrels. The Lord's servant must not quarrel, but must be gentle to everyone, able to teach, and patient, instructing his opponents with gentleness." 2 Timothy 2:22-25

Reject foolish and ignorant disputes.

Because when we decide to have disagreements with one another that are foolish or ignorant, we are creating unnecessary dissension among His people.

We were all made uniquely, and disputes will arise. God calls us to speak from a place of gentleness to everyone. Companions and opponents.

From this disposition we can present ourselves in a manner that is pleasing to God and reflects the tenderness that He shows us daily through His love, mercy and grace.

We weren't created to make others feel less than, left out, demeaned or have a "You can't sit with us" attitude.

We were created to build a longer table and sit with our brothers and sisters in Christ who together want to pursue a faithful life accepting His peace in all circumstances and being okay with the uncomfortable.

We don't get to write out the invitations for who gets to sit at the table with Jesus. There is a place there for everyone.

We have this warped view of love because we live in the world.

God's love is uncomfortable but it's the most genuine love we will ever experience. It's because love isn't all fuzzy feelings. God's love is the example of bringing out the best in each one of us.

The sons and daughters of God are broken people.

We can choose to use our example of worldly love and seek out the comfortable. We can only sit with the people who make us feel warm, cozy and good about ourselves. We can reject the people we don't understand. We can create a bubble around ourselves so that we play it safe.

Or we can choose the way God loves and lay down our pride to step into the uncomfortable. We can sit with the people who make us feel good about ourselves *and* with the people who challenge us. We can welcome in everyone and choose to figure out how God has created everyone differently to fulfill His purpose in a way you aren't able to.

I invite you to pop the bubble.

We all can't look the same, do the same, be the same.

We are in this for THE common purpose— to glorify God.

The routes we take to do that are different.

The giftings we are all given to do that are different.

The experiences we have went through to do that are different.

The passions we are all given to do that are different.

The personalities we have all been provided with to do that are different.

Our differences do not divide us.

We can try to box people in by those differences and decide that the differences between us are too uncomfortable to deal with or we can decide to see what God sees in them.

He doesn't see division. He sees an army of people with the exact skill sets, mindsets, passions, knowledge and capability to rise up strongly together. He sees a diverse people who have access to different communities, social groups and platforms. He sees the opportunity for the army to swoop into the various populations to spread His Truth far and wide.

If we want to continue to grant people permission to embrace their callings, we must choose to quit dividing ourselves because of surface level judgments.

If we want to weave into every part of this world to not just impact people, but radically change them with the love of Christ, we must choose to see the strengths and abilities of one another to reach the masses.

If we want to serve Him to our fullest capacity, we must step into the uncomfortable, shoulder to shoulder with people who aren't afraid to lay down comparison for the challenge of a battle bigger than themselves.

When it comes to our social media feeds, what if we decided to see how other people have a different ability to reach a different pocket of people that you don't have access to?

What if we decided to view their posts as connecting factors to cultivate a community you can't create because your passions are different?

What if we decided to understand that what they do, if done in love and purpose, isn't meant to make you find a reason to have a dispute with them, but instead a way to diversify?

What if instead we asked for new eyes to see social media as an avenue for His gain and not for our own comfort?

The world is vast, and we need to lay down our comfort for the uncomfortable that God calls us into together.

This breaks the chains of becoming known for your own gain.

Social media isn't yours to control to collect applause.

When we link arms in our common purpose and choose to see how our differences make us powerful together, social media is a massive avenue to reach our brothers and sisters and let God's glory be known.

We like to blame social media for the demise of our society, but broken people will create hurt anywhere.

We need to end the blame game and widen our focus to the bigger picture.

It's time to connect with intention instead of unfriending in disagreement.

I am in the belief that anything can be used for evil if it is manipulated in that way, but I also believe that we have the higher power of righteousness on our side in order to give power to anything for good. This includes social media. I believe that this platform can be used for His good to build the Kingdom of God.

I also know that many will fight the battle, will lose and won't come back. It is a lot to take when the world attacks, when Satan places a target upon your back, when he decides you are too much of a potential threat.

But we are not the world's people.

We are God's.

When we decide to completely embrace the fact that we are not of the world, we have a renewed faith and ability to restore the things in our world so that others can also come to understand His truth and His goodness. His love will shine through us if we decide to fight the battle of social media. If we decide to take a stand and not allow the world to overcome us.

I choose to continue interacting with others on social media. I choose to be a positive presence in the social media world. I choose to fight the battle even when Satan attacks, because I know that when Satan is attacking, I am doing good. When I am a threat that means I am doing something right. It means the Devil is scared to death of what I am bringing to the people he intends to shackle for life and drag to his own domain in hell.

I serve a risen Savior who in the end claims victory. His very name echoes victory.

You serve a risen Savior whose name echoes victory.

Soak that in for a second.

Your losses are simply inconveniences. They may seem like inconveniences for you, but they especially are for Satan, because his energy was spent battling you instead of shackling others in chains.

Suit up.

Choose to be a freedom fighter. There are way too many people who are out there crying out for freedom in this world and yes, in this world of social media. It is a battlefield and you are needed. We are all needed together.

Social media is part of the world we live in and although we do not want to conform to the world, what would happen if all the good people left social media because it got too hard? Because it was a battle? Because when you'd take two steps forward, you'd get punched a step back?

What would social media become?

We have an obligation to shine His light and there is great hurt on social media platforms. We need to be interacting there. We need to be a presence. We need to shine truth and love.

We must show up which means we have to have a social media account.

In doing this, we also must realize we are in deep need of putting on the full armor of God, because we are about to face battles of the world that are aimed directly at our heart, which could also cause the selfishness in us to rise up just because of the platform we are fighting on.

The devil is present. Where people are, he will be there. He is here to convince us of sinful ways and to distract us from the freedom, love, joy, and purpose that is found in God.

Social media is the perfect breeding ground for comparison, the perfect breeding ground for fears of insecurity, the perfect breeding ground for selfishness, and the perfect breeding ground for hatred.

Finally, be strengthened by the Lord and by his vast strength. Put on the full armor of God so that you can stand against the schemes of the devil. For our struggle is not against flesh and blood, but against the rulers, against the authorities, against the cosmic powers of this darkness, against evil spiritual forces in the heavens. For this reason take up the full armor of God, so that you may be able to resist in the evil day, and having prepared everything, to take your stand. Stand, therefore, with truth like a belt around your waist, righteousness like armor on your chest, and your feet sandaled with readiness for the gospel of peace. In every situation take up the shield of faith with which you can extinguish all the flaming arrows of the evil one. Take the helmet of salvation and the sword of the Spirit---which is the word of God. Pray at all times in the Spirit with every prayer and request, and stay alert with all perseverance and intercession for all the saints. Ephesians 6:10-18

Stand. Have faith. Persevere. Intercede.

Social media needs you to drop the need for being known by the world so that you are not snagged into a worldly trap of despair and selfishness. Social media needs you to take a stand, humble yourself, persevere when it gets hard, and have faith that God is going to show up big in your life so that you are used to intercede in the lives of others. Social media needs you to rally together with others in a common purpose to glorify His name.

This is no easy task, but it is a task that we are called to do, so that the brokenness of the world can be healed by the love of God.

We need to ask God to light up our lives.

We need to ask God to light up our paths.

We need to ask God to light up our opportunities.

We need God, so we can light up the social media world with His goodness and His peace.

We can't deny that social media is an integral part of our present and part of our future. We need to ignite it with His love through us, through our presence, through our posts.

We can be the encouragers, the overcomers, the people that make social media a brighter place instead of a world of darkness.

We must leave our old habits and our old needs of being known behind. We must walk forward with new intentions to use social media for His good instead of our own.

In this way we will eliminate our need for being known in the world of people and instead allow Him to be known within us.

We live for Him, not for the world.

Once we can align our priorities of social media with the priorities of what we are called to do in this life, we will find a harmonious balance that has us desiring the interactions from Him instead of the social media interactions of the world.

Again, this is not easy, but I believe it is necessary that we fight the good fight in all realms of our life.

There are times in our social media lives that we will need tactics in order to help ourselves keep from succumbing to works of our flesh. It's okay to have a toolbox to help yourself out.

So, let's go through a few tools for the toolbox.

A trick I have learned that helps me focus on the fact that social media is a tool, is to simply not pick up my phone and scroll until I've began my day. By picking up our phones in the morning and immediately going to social media, we didn't take the time to put on our full armor. We didn't take the time to prepare our hearts and minds for what we would stumble upon in our newsfeed.

Breaks are necessary sometimes. Whether it is 3 days, a week or a month, breaks can be completely refreshing. They allow you to come back with renewed focus on your God-given callings and not the purposes that you've attached yourself to that are of the world.

So, feel free to take breaks. Unchain your emotions from the stats of your status updates and dig into His Word to break your soul free from the expectations of the world.

Another tactic that I like to utilize is the "unfollow" button.

Notice I said "unfollow", not "unfriend". That unfriending button can be utilized when some spammy account happens, but the "unfriend" button can actually cause more issues than freedom.

Why do I say that?

Unfriending someone, unless you have absolute just reason, is not necessarily displaying the fruits of the Spirit. Listen, I get that you might believe that is a stretch, but it really isn't.

I've been unfriended. Many times. Most times, I don't understand why.

I'll see their name pop up on someone else's feed and think "Oh! I haven't seen their content for a while now!" and then I'll click on them and realize that I'm not their friend anymore.

The fruits of the Spirit are love, joy, peace, patience, kindness, goodness, faithfulness, gentleness and self-control.

If you unfriend someone because of any works of the flesh, that's on you and not on them. It isn't working within the fruits of the Spirit but instead within the works of yourself.

If you are trying to protect yourself from the issues of comparison and rid yourself of a social media addiction, the "unfollow" button works just fine. Then when you have relinquished the control of your emotions against the comparison of others, you can follow them back. That way they have no knowledge you were struggling with comparing yourself to them and you avoid causing them hurt from unfriending them.

I've had to unfollow a handful of people during different comparison seasons of my life and I can now follow them without strife. Yes, I was bitter towards some of my now really great friends.

Now, it's possible that you have been unfriended as well and maybe you carry that heavily upon your shoulders as I have been known to do. When this happens, I simply tell myself it is on them and not on me. I can't afford to carry the burden of someone else's unique journey. So, if you have been hurt by the "unfriend" button, release yourself of any guilt you may feel from it. Then remind yourself how the "unfriend" button feels and if an "unfriend" isn't necessary but an "unfollow" may be, use your judgment wisely. We want to create a space of peace and love, not a place that disrupts harmony and causes hurt. There is enough guilt and shame that the world puts on us without us being used to create that kind of hurt.

Another way that may be helpful for you to utilize in creating a better social media situation is to simply delete the apps off of your phone. This makes social media a little less distracting without the constant updates, which can keep you from comparing and attaching your emotions to checking your notifications waiting for people to show up. It also keeps you from scrolling aimlessly, wasting the time you could be utilizing for other things you need to be doing to work towards your God-given purpose.

You can still check social media, however, having to go to your computer or a tablet makes it a little less addictive as you aren't carrying your social media status around in your pocket all day long.

Setting time limits for yourself that work within your own personal schedule, can be helpful. Whether you realize that you need to log off when your kids and spouse are home, in the evenings, whenever you find yourself wasting the most time, or during times where you are vulnerable to your emotions, get off your social media.

Feel free to customize your toolbox with the tools that work for you.

Sometimes we simply need to detach ourselves from our social media so that we can relearn how to attach ourselves to the things that truly matter in our lives. Detaching ourselves doesn't mean that we don't show up or that we don't post transparently. It simply means that we are not defined by who shows up on our feeds or how we measure up to someone else's.

Once we begin to seek freedom in using our social media as a tool and controlling it as such, we can finally release the control that social media has over our emotions, our actions, and our thoughts.

Social media does not have to dictate how you live your life by constantly trying to keep up and creating content for people to show up. Social media does not have to define who you are. Social media gets to be a resource that you are able to use to show others how Christ is working freely through you. You have freed yourself from how social media was controlling you.

When you are able to do this, it allows you to fight for His Kingdom instead of fighting for your own causes. When you surrender your life in every aspect, God shows up to fight for you.

We selfishly spend our time waiting for others to show up for us on social media and He has been there all along ready to show up for you in every way that you need Him to. He's got you. He's there for you. He's the only "love" reaction that truly needs to show up in your life.

We are the overcomers. The world shakers. The truth seekers and the truth tellers.

If we want to impact the world and shake up its' ideas, we need to be present, and we need to be on the offense instead of on the defense. This means we happen to social media; it does not happen to us.

We need to prepare ourselves. We need to suit up. We need to be what the social media world needs now for the people who desperately need us to show up.

Prepare yourself for battle, friend.

-5-

WHO ARE YOU KNOWN BY?

To be fully known, we must dive into Who we are fully known by.

Who is this Creator that bravely claims us as His own creation?

Who is this Father who pulls us up on His lap as His children with gentleness, when we've been disobedient and feel like we've completely lost our way?

God—his way is perfect; the word of the Lord is pure. He is a shield to all who take refuge in him. For who is God besides the Lord? And who is a rock? Only our God. Psalm 18:30-31

I love the word refuge in reference to who God is to us.

I've grown up incredibly fortunate to have an earthly father that I massively adore. To this day I don't believe there isn't something my daddy can't do. It drove my mother crazy because my sister and I would always side with our dad. We knew he wasn't perfect, but we viewed him as our refuge. He was our safety.

I crumpled anytime I thought I had disappointed him. I didn't want to let him down. I wanted him to always be proud of me.

We had human fathers discipline us, and we respected them. Shouldn't we submit even more to the Father of spirits and live? For they disciplined us for a short time based on what seemed good to them, but he does it for our benefit, so that we can share his holiness.

Hebrews 12: 9-10

Our Father in Heaven is perfect. He is our safety. He is love. He is holy.

When we walk out the trampled, worn out path of the world we begin to question the definition of God and His truth. We begin to attempt to redefine Who He is, when we would prefer chasing God down on our own terms instead of walking toward Him on His.

However, that isn't how the relationship with our Father in Heaven works. In fact, my earthly father would have disciplined me if I decided to come to him with my own rules instead of his own.

"I know I wasn't supposed to be over at his house tonight dad, but it felt like a better choice for me, so I went ahead and decided it was okay."

If I said the above, it probably wouldn't have gone over incredibly well with my dad.

Our Heavenly Father wants us to be obedient and make decisions that align with His ways and not our own.

The good news is He doesn't leave us here on earth without the opportunity to equip ourselves.

He left us with His Word.

All Scripture is inspired by God and is profitable for teaching, for rebuking, for correcting, for training in righteousness, so that the man of God may be complete, equipped for every good work. 2 Timothy 3:16-17

When I was younger the Bible greatly intimidated me.

It wasn't necessarily because of the magnitude of it, but because every time I read the Bible I was convicted in some area of my life. I didn't want to recognize that God's discipline was an aspect of God's love.

As adults wandering through the mess that is our current world, we don't always like to open God's Word and be corrected. Medicine doesn't always taste good to an ailing patient.

My sister despised medicine growing up.

I remember her locking herself inside the bathroom with her little medicine cup of vibrant colored syrup and secretly pouring it down the drain. She would then quietly wash it down with a slow stream of water from the faucet.

We don't always like the idea that what we need is something that may not taste good or feel good. It's easier to only listen, but not truly absorb it. Then we go a step further and water it down.

We use the Bible like my sister used the medicine cup. The appearance of taking it in and then watering it down to hide the evidence of the actual medicine we needed.

But be doers of the word and not hearers only, deceiving yourselves. James 1:22

We need to wade through the Word so deeply that our feet cannot touch the ground. This creates a dependence on the promise that God will make us stronger in our faith through immersing ourselves in Who He is and who He is making us.

Our offensive hearts need to surrender up the pride that creates a desire for worldly lies, over the truth of His Word.

We have shortcomings and that is okay. It is not okay to use our shortcomings as an excuse to not want to recognize truth.

The shortcomings that allow us to buy into the belief that our social media accounts determine our worth and success. The shortcomings that immerse us within the ideals and lies of the world instead of believing in His promises. The shortcomings that create us to blur our understanding of truth when we choose to please people instead of looking up and ask what is pleasing to God.

We need to take a different path to rediscover His truth. We need to step off the path where we are trained to water down truth in order to make it appealing to others.

We are being trained through the Scripture, through the working of the Spirit and through the experiences God creates for us in order to grow.

Listen friend, if you are serious about your training in order to become equipped properly for your purpose of glorifying His name, there is not a person you can listen to on a podcast, a post you can read on your newsfeed, or a book you can pick up that will give you the tools necessary like the Bible will.

For the time will come when people will not tolerate sound doctrine, but according to their own desires, will multiply teachers for themselves because they have an itch to hear what they want to hear. 2 Timothy 4:3

Podcasts are good. Books are good. Facebook Lives are good.

All ways can be used to glorify God and can be good.

However, the problem with only learning about God through the mouths of other people and not from the actual Word of God, is that it can be wrapped up in a worldly opinion that is not true.

Discernment is important when you are choosing people to listen to. There are multiple references in the Bible about false teachings because teachers have decided to give people what they want to feel more comfortable.

We need to stop tiptoeing around His Word scared it may cause us to become rejected by others. We need to stop using scripture as our social media cover photo like a band-aid over our brokenness, believing that is enough. We need to choose to drink deeply from The Word and radically change our lives because the same truth that was applicable hundreds of years ago stands true today.

The Bible doesn't change. People change. Society changes. Politics change. Worldly standards are constantly evolving. The Word is the same yesterday, today and tomorrow. It is a constant in our world that only continues to change.

The world will reject you for it.

In fact, all who want to live a godly life in Christ Jesus will be persecuted. 2 Timothy 3:12

When you pursue God in your life, you will not always be applauded for it. In fact, you will be rejected many times.

Rejection by people hurts. It is sometimes difficult to choose that life on purpose.

For the longest time I carried around this expectation of rejection.

It was a learned behavior created from past friends abandoning me in times of need to join those that were attacking me. As we learned with our past, sometimes we hold onto negative behaviors that keep us from pressing deeply into Whose we are in Christ.

Expecting rejection was one of mine.

When I moved into a community with a fresh start of new women, I was hopeful to be accepted for simply being me. Moving into new areas is difficult enough, but I had this anticipation of rejection because I'd never experienced one of those female friendships where they truly had your back in any situation.

I craved those connections but didn't know how to make them.

I didn't want to create a facade to be accepted either. I wanted to be accepted for me.

I held my breath in every conversation praying I wasn't messing it up.

But rejection eventually came.

He was despised and rejected by men, a man of suffering who knew what sickness was. He was like someone people turned away from; he was despised, and we didn't value him.

Yet he himself bore our sickness, and he carried our pains;

But we in turn regarded him stricken, struck down by God, and afflicted.

But he was pierced because of our rebellion, crushed because of our iniquities; punishment for our peace was on him, and we are healed by his wound.

We all went astray like sheep; we all have turned to our own way; and the Lord has punished him for the iniquity of us all.

Isaiah 53:3-6

Our ability to have peace despite rejection, was given to us on that cross.

When we choose to be silent in Whose we are because we fear rejection, we harshly underestimate the ability we were given through the death of our Savior.

Jesus was critically rejected.

Jesus felt our pain. Not just our physical pains, but our emotional ones too.

People did not see His worth and people are sometimes going to look over your worth too.

He felt what we feel so He could carry it and give us the opportunity to be free from rejection, from hurt, from our iniquities.

We are already cured from the pains of the world, if we choose to remove our desires from the ways of the world.

This doesn't mean we won't experience rejection, pain, shame, or any broken feeling of this world, it simply means we are not owned by it.

We live in a dying world and we will experience the dying world. Jesus lived as the perfect man and not even He avoided the pains of the dying world.

The perfect man rejected.

The perfect man enduring all pain.

The perfect man choosing the difficult path over the "free and easy" one the world offers.

The perfect man exampling to us how to approach our Heavenly Father hundreds of years later through His example written in the Word of God.

The path of holiness is not a path exempt from struggle. It's a path with a promise that your struggles are simply a dot on a sentence in the story of His glory and redemption in your life.

The truth is not a trap. The truth sets you free.

But you are a chosen race, a royal priesthood, a holy nation, a people for his possession, so that you may proclaim the praises of the one who called you out of darkness into his marvelous light. 1 Peter 2:9

Do you know why you are chosen? Why you are worthy of being clothed as royalty?

Let's back it up a bit.

Therefore, rid yourselves of all malice, all deceit, hypocrisy, envy and all slander. Like newborn infants, desire the pure milk of the word, so that you may grow up in your salvation, if you have tasted that the Lord is good. As you come to him, a living stone—rejected by people but chosen and honored by God—you yourselves, as living stones, a spiritual house, are being built to be a holy priesthood to offer spiritual sacrifices acceptable to God through Jesus Christ. 1 Peter 2:1-5

Rejected by people but **chosen** and **honored** by God. Why? Because you rid yourselves of the worldly ways in exchange for ways that are holy, good, and pleasing to God.

There are two kinds of people.

People of the worldly kingdom and people of the Lord's Kingdom.

When we choose to place our value in who we are because of whose we are instead of who the world says we are, we begin to welcome our own rejection of the world. We enter our place in the Lord's Kingdom.

It sounds simple, but it is a path that is difficult to walk out because we are also rejecting the broken lies the world murmurs to us frequently. We have been accustomed to the lies about us.

You aren't enough.

You aren't worthy of being more than you are right now.

You're not even worthy of what you are now.

People don't like you as much as they like others.

(unfriend button pushed)

What do you even have to offer?

Are you qualified?

What makes you special?

You aren't truly needed.

No one will ever love you.

I've had most of these said to me, but I allowed the last phrase to hold me in bondage longer than I even realized.

One phrase. Six words. They aren't complex but they held power because I allowed power to rest in a person, instead of what the Lord has already spoken over me.

When it comes to our social media experience, we are given multiple opportunities to see how the world wants to offer something completely opposite to us. We absently absorb as we scroll.

We make our own choices. We can take the path of the worldly lies—in either that we are enough on our own or that we will never be enough as everyone else on our newsfeed.

I've swam in my inadequacies, treading water hoping that someone would see me and throw me a life preserver.

We know that we should not place our worth in the hands of others, but we do so because we long for being loved, accepted, and admired. When it comes to social media, being loved by others equates to how often they push the "like" button. Sure, it feels good and it looks good, but it isn't where our focus should be when determining if our friends are going to show up for us. We shouldn't even be worrying about whether our friends will show up for us at all, because God has already shown up for us a multitude of times. He is the only one standing in the end that truly matters.

So why is this so difficult for us to do?

We desire for our darkness to be exposed by His light so that we never have to feel shadowed by our sins again.

We are conditioned.

We have been truly trained to believe the lies of the world about ourselves. Even when we know deep down, what the Lord says about us. We slip into our habits of believing the lies of shame, inadequacy, disappointment, disqualifications, unworthiness, and all the areas we feel we lack in our life.

We've created this path of thinking, that when we experience rejection or comparison, we immediately walk the path of destructive lies we've allowed the world to tell us over time.

Conditioned. Trained. It is learned.

What does this mean?

We can retrain ourselves and create a new habit so when we experience rejection or comparison, we can walk a new path paved out of His Truths about us.

Let's repeat this part again.

Like newborn infants, desire the pure milk of the word, so that you may grow up in your salvation, if you have tasted that the Lord is good. As you come to him, a living stone—rejected by people but chosen and honored by God......1 Peter 2:2-4A

When we dig into His Word with the desire like a newborn desires milk, we will grow up in our salvation. Our salvation is our redemption, our deliverance, our rescue or our recovery. Our recovery from the ways of this world, from the lies we have previously consumed. We were truly drinking from the wrong source of milk. We were trying to quench ourselves with the resources of the world, instead of consuming what we were truly thirsting for.

This is the best news!

We can retrain our brains and our habits by making the choice to read His Word often.

Earlier I said that I used to be intimidated by the Bible.

It's large. The thousands upon thousands of words to read and try to comprehend can make you anxious.

We don't need to memorize the Bible from cover to cover, we simply need to be in it. We need to be consuming it more than we consume the words of the world.

I decided I needed to make reading the Bible easier for me.

I, first, released myself of the thought process of memorization. I do feel memorization is important when you need to equip yourself with verses of His Truth, but we shouldn't allow it to detour us from being in His Word.

Secondly, I just open the Bible.

No reading plans.

I tell myself at some point between 8 a.m. and 9 a.m. every morning, I need to open and read. Sometimes I read a chapter or sometimes I read a book during the entire day because I become obsessed with the story.

We don't need to make this complicated. We need to allow ourselves the opportunity for His Word to wash over our hearts and our minds with to free us from the lies of the world.

While we are discussing lies of the world, let's dive into some other ones that aren't necessarily about us as a person, but are lies that tell us how to succeed in this world.

This is important because we have also been conditioned that our worth is found in our worldly success. Kingdom success is much different than worldly success.

Hustle until you no longer have to introduce yourself.

The true success is in the person who invented himself.

Sacrifice comes before success.

Success is awesome. I'm not going to deny that. I love to cheer my friends on when they succeed at something they've been working diligently on, and I love when my friends cheer me on too.

It isn't the success that is negative. It's the path taken towards success and the attitude towards it that can keep us from staying in alignment with God's desire for our lives.

How happy is the one who does not walk in the advice of the wicked or stand in the pathway with sinners or sit in the company of mockers! Instead, his delight is in the Lord's instruction, and he meditates on it day and night. He is like a tree planted beside flowing streams that bears its fruit in its season and whose leaf does not wither. Whatever he does prospers. Psalm 1:1-3

A prosperous, successful life in the eyes of the Lord is rooted in the truth of His Word.

As your roots grow deeper in your faith through your obedience in being in the Word, and you firmly ground yourself in His righteousness, the success you achieve in your life isn't based on your own merit. This allows you to fully comprehend where prosperity overflows from—God.

The world offers up a lot of advice when it comes to achieving success, but it also does not guarantee success to all who work for it.

Kingdom success is not reserved for a certain few.

Kingdom success is beyond worldly understanding, because it was purchased through the sacrifice and phenomenon of the resurrection.

God allows you to find peace in your life as you plant yourself beside His stream of living water that gives you something the world cannot—everlasting life.

Worldly success doesn't get the chance to own you or define you when you root in deep to Whose you truly are in Him.

God wants you to prosper.

God wants you to live fully.

God wants you to feel loved because the truest definition of love rests in who He is.

For God loved the world in this way: He gave his one and only Son, so that everyone who believes in him will not perish but have eternal life. For God did not send his Son to condemn the world, but to save the world through him. John 3:16-17

It wasn't the nails that held Christ to the cross. It was love. Love kept him on that cross in order to set you free.

God loves you so much that He did not want to be separated from you. The separation through your sins would have kept you from eternal life with Him, but the bridge was built through the death of Christ. Jesus took your brokenness so that you could be made whole.

You are known by a Father who cares deeply for the person you are, the person you were, and the person you are becoming.

When you begin digging deep into Whose you are, will discover that your desire for a relationship with your Father grows.

So then, just as you have received Christ Jesus as Lord, continue to live in him, being rooted and built up in him and established in the faith, just as you were taught, and overflowing with gratitude.

Colossians 2: 6-7

You will continue to learn more about Who you are known by, as you continue to root yourself in His Truth and build your life through God.

How thankful I am that I can grow in my relationship with my Father! I am free to live because I am truly free in the One who deeply knows me.

-6-

EMBRACING YOUR GIFTS

*For you are saved by grace through faith, and this is not from yourselves;
it is God's gift—not from works, so that no one can boast. For we are
his workmanship, created in Christ Jesus for good works, which God
prepared ahead of time for us to do. Ephesians 2:8-10*

Nothing we prepare from our hands would have ever been
enough to save us. We are not in competition for a spot in
Heaven. He isn't weighing good deeds versus good deeds.
There is no roster and only so many spots. Our salvation is
God's gift through the sacrifice of His Son on the cross.

Even though we are not saved through our good works, God
cared enough for each of us to prepare good works ahead to
fulfill purpose. Our good works would never save us, but
they may lead others to the gift of redemption.

Soak that in for a second.

When you choose to use your gifting to fulfill the good works
God has prepared for you, you may lead someone to
salvation through Jesus Christ.

Our God is not a God of accident. He is a God of purpose and He has already authored the qualities and characteristics you need to fulfill your purpose here on earth. When we choose to tap into His intention, we choose to tap into His goodness that is planned so beautifully and intentionally for our lives.

Our rebellious hearts need to focus on His intention for our lives.

A rebel heart only delays His goodness.

In a world where we want to be known, a rebel heart tends to look for ways that allow ourselves to be seen and known by others. We chase actions that look good, feel good, and that appear to serve a purpose. We chase the action that the world will see. We chase the action that the world will applaud. Sometimes we will label the action saying that it is part of "His plan" to make it look even better.

But friend, it isn't better.

When we have a small view of God and a big view of self, we blind ourselves to the ways we can be used for His Kingdom.

We chase status for our good works. We want people to see us creating a movement. We want to #hashtag our life so people watch the things we are doing.

The problem is that sometimes we chase these movements and actions, then attach our purpose to them when we were created for something else.

Worldly movements can sometimes be distractions from Kingdom movement.

You see, God created a redemption movement thousands of years ago. We don't have to recreate purpose. We need to figure out how we are supposed to be used for His Kingdom movement.

He gave us ways to live out life in this world, without being of it.

We were given callings. Different callings. Same callings. Callings that even when similar look different because of personality, experience, passion, and gifts.

The uniqueness of people was created with reason. God's got an action plan. God is never surprised.

I chose you before I formed you in the womb; I set you apart before you were born. Jeremiah 1:5a

Jeremiah was appointed a prophet by God. He was chosen and set apart before he even arrived earth-side. When he was told this, he protested. Being chosen by God is a great responsibility. But, being chosen by God is also an incredible honor.

How are you honoring God with your life?

Are you using the gifts He gave you to fulfill the Kingdom purpose you were created for? Are you using your gifts for your own gain instead of His? Are you even using your gifts at all?

Just like Jeremiah, you are chosen and set apart.

In our world of social media, we are sometimes tempted with chasing down the gifts that other people have. I know I've done this. Other people's gifts sometimes look better, are accepted, create status, welcome in applause through "likes", and just make them appear greater.

I've charged forward trying to imitate others that were created differently.

The problem is when we forge ahead because we see that our status could be elevated by using gifts that aren't ours, we will come across more obstacles to deter us because we were not created to operate in that way.

It is the equivalent of trying to run a marathon if you were gifted with the ability to short distance sprint. You can train all day, every day, with the intent of becoming a marathon runner. You can put in the hours and experience the pain. You can do the same runs to prepare as a gifted marathon runner. You can buy the same product to support your body as a marathon runner. However, when the marathon happens and you find yourself competing against those that train **and** are naturally gifted in it, they will do better.

Now if you had been out there putting in the same effort and determination in becoming the best short distance sprinter, and you are naturally gifted in short distance sprinting, you are going to amazingly succeed in a competitive sprint.

Operating outside your gifting creates a deficit in your attempt from the beginning.

This isn't meant to make you feel like you are not enough. It is quite the opposite. God created you enough in your own arena. If you are operating within your own gifts you will outwork anyone who is operating outside of theirs because you were **made** for it. You were purposely shaped, molded, and intricately designed to succeed with your own gifting.

Not everyone will accept your gifting, either.

My oldest daughter is a quiet force that owns the gifts within her.

She knows she is creative. She knows she is kind. She also knows not everyone is going to like her.

She came home from school one day and we were discussing how to display kindness, even when someone isn't the most kind in the classroom. She looked at me and she said, "Some people say mean things about me. I just take the good and ignore the bad, because the bad isn't true."

I think I sat there for at least a minute, stunned, mouth wide open.

At the age of 5, she has already learned something that it took me well into my 20's to firmly grasp.

You will never please everyone, but you weren't meant to adapt the person you were created to become so others were accepting of you.

Not everyone is going to be happy for you. Not everyone is going to see your gifts and think they are amazing. Not everyone is going to surround you in encouragement and support. Not everyone is going to like who you are.

Someone once told me my thoughts were better left in a journal.

Someone once shared one of my posts I wrote along with their own nasty words in obvious disagreement.

Someone once told me that I wasn't qualified to go forward in what I wanted to pursue, because I had no experience.

At some point in our life, we begin to lose security in who we are and replace it with the insecurities in who we aren't. We buy into the lies others speak over us. We are compared with others when we didn't ask to be compared in the first place.

I remember when I was younger overhearing a conversation between adults. I'm sure they didn't mean to trigger an insecurity within myself, but as a young, impressionable girl, I unfortunately took it to heart.

It was over my outwardly appearance.

As an elementary girl, I admittedly would tell you that I was very much awkward. I liked layered clothes, wearing butterfly clips, and had those tiny little glasses that only covered your eyeballs.

I remember hearing these adults say how, although I was cute, I wasn't as cute as another little girl.

Their words were in their own conversation, but being indirectly apart of it opened my eyes to this idea that I wasn't as pretty as someone else. It made me look at my awkwardness and feel like I was holding up a bright neon sign announcing my weirdness. I suddenly felt like I was in competition.

I was in fifth grade.

There is a time in our life where we begin to absorb the lies that the world tells us.

You aren't pretty enough.

You aren't smart enough.

You aren't talented enough.

You aren't skinny enough.

You aren't loved enough.

You aren't liked enough.

You will never be enough.

We begin to obsess about our "lack of" instead of celebrating our "strong in". These ongoing comparisons we've made over the years can build up. This overflows into our social media interactions where we will often think of ourselves in competition. This competition keeps us from truly embracing the gifts that we have been given by our Father.

We don't want to admit how juvenile our actions and thoughts seem when it comes to our comparison on social media. When I've asked friends how they feel about revealing where they struggle with social media, I always feel shame within their words when they describe the details of how it affects them.

Friend, we distract ourselves with the small workings of social media.

Why do we make ourselves feel inadequate? The definition of inadequate is insufficient for a purpose. But we know we were chosen for purpose.

When we allow comparison in...

When we long for validation from others...

When we focus on our lacks instead of our strengths in our gifts...

When we allow people's words and actions to control our emotions...

We will spiral into believing that we are not enough to step into a position where we are used for His glory.

You are not inadequate. Jesus did not die for you to feel inadequacy.

Jesus overcame this world **for us,** so our inadequacies were washed away by the mighty love and grace of God.

We keep ourselves from truly embracing Whose we are and who we were created to become, when we constantly subject ourselves to a thought process that informs us—we don't measure up.

God is the only One who knows what you were made for.

The world will continue to label you for the rest of your life. Those labels hold no worth.

God is the one Who defines you.

One morning, standing in my bathroom, I was fighting doubts battling within my head. Who was I to believe that I could write a book? Who was I to believe that my words would make a difference? There were so many writers out there who were already producing amazing pieces, with so much more experience than I had. Who was I?

I heard a gentle, but strong voice.

I am rising up a new generation.

A new generation. The next generation.

God constantly needs His people to rise up to fulfill His Kingdom plans. There isn't a maximum number placed on how many are able to rise up. He needs people who constantly answer the call, who boldly step forward, and who humbly say, "Send me".

We were created for this time. We were created to rise up. We were created to be part of the movement to build His Kingdom.

There are millions of writers, that doesn't mean you shouldn't write.

There are millions of teachers, that doesn't mean you shouldn't teach.

There are millions of speakers, that doesn't mean you shouldn't speak.

Your gifts are needed now and were intentional from the very beginning, before you even drew your first breath in this world.

We do not need to be validated by other people in order to have permission to forge ahead in our own gifts. God validated those gifts already. No explanation is required.

For by the grace given to me, I tell everyone among you not to think of himself more highly than he should think. Instead, think sensibly, as God has distributed a measure of faith to each one. Now as we have many parts in one body, and all parts do not have the same function, in the same way we who are many are one body in Christ and individually members of one another. According to the grace given to us, we have different gifts: If prophecy, use it according to the proportion of one's faith; if service, us it in service; if teaching, in teaching; if exhorting, in exhortation; giving, with generosity; leading, with diligence; showing mercy, with cheerfulness. Romans 12: 3-7

There are many gifts. We were all called to go forward differently in our lives to serve the greater purpose of glorifying His name. God desires us to dig in and figure out how He uniquely created each one of us.

When God was focused on creating the person that you would become, He was installing different, beautiful pieces within you that would set you apart from others. He was intentionally creating you to be unique with the ability to do amazing things. He wants you to live life fully.

We are the hands and feet of Christ. We are the ones moving our feet and extending our hands to reach the people in this world who need Jesus.

That is why we are equipped.

Not only do we have His Word, His strength and victory over death—we have the tools needed to save the ones who have been shadowed by the devil's darkness.

When it comes to social media and using your gift, it doesn't matter if you impacted 1 person or 10,000.

Quit comparing your gifts to the gifts of others.

Quit desiring the gifts of others.

Quit operating outside of your gifts.

Embrace the gifts that you have so purposely been given. You were designed intentionally. God makes no mistakes. You are a masterpiece.

-7-

SEASONS AND CIRCUMSTANCES

I want to begin this chapter with an understanding that social media is not mentioned heavily through these words. Why?

What you see on social media is such a small part of someone's life. This is so important for us to recognize, because the day to day we each are walking out, needs to be accounted for when we are scrolling our social media feeds.

We each navigate different seasons and circumstances in our lives. We need to do better to remember that what we see on our feeds, does not give us all the details.

Now let's figure out why seasons and circumstances are vital for embracing Whose we are.

The story of Leah and Rachel rocked my world one Thursday morning during my time in the Word. I wouldn't stay quiet about it. Date night with my husband was riddled with so many different takeaways from the story of Leah and Rachel.

My husband and I were out to dinner and I was asking, "Can you imagine if you were in love with my sister and you were tricked into sleeping with me to become your wife? I mean the sister rivalry."

He replied with his logical thinking, "No, because I wouldn't have wanted to marry your sister."

It was a story I've heard before, but I'd never explored it in the way I did that day.

It wasn't just the deceit from the beginning.

It intrigued me that Leah and Rachel were both handed unfortunate circumstances. Leah, hated. She married the man who loved her younger sister through deceit created by their father. It angered Jacob that he had been duped and he worked out another deal so he could still marry Rachel and when he did...

Jacob slept with Rachel also, and indeed, he loved Rachel more than Leah. Genesis 29:30

He loved her more. She was the beloved. However, there's more.

When the Lord saw that Leah was unloved, he opened her womb; but Rachel was unable to conceive. Genesis 29:31

I think it is important to note that God created these circumstances. It wasn't Satan that made Rachel barren or created a situation of hate for Leah.

We tend to give too much credit to Satan in our circumstances. Whenever we feel opposition, challenge, or something that feels incredibly difficult in our life, we tend to say, "Not today Satan". We think anything uncomfortable must come from him.

It isn't that Satan doesn't engage in war against us. He does. He is always looking for opportunity to darken us and keep us from fulfilling our Kingdom intentions. But when we believe that our Father Who loves us dearly, Who created us with purpose, and Who has gone before us, oversees our lives, we cannot so easily surrender up an uncomfortable time in our life to the credit of Satan.

There is discipline in the Bible, friend. Lots and lots of discipline.

As a parent, I better understand this. With love comes discipline. I want my children to go through experience to learn how to live life well. I want them to walk through circumstances that allow them to grow. I want them to discover their purpose. That requires not sheltering them from all disappointment and hurt in their lives.

Our Father does the same. He doesn't want us to live a worldly mediocre, so He gives us situations in which we can be molded into the person we were created to become in His greatness. He wants us to learn through the circumstances that create a journey of a well-lived life. He doesn't want us searching for a hand out but instead reaching for His hand to pull us up.

Let's take the city of Jerusalem and the book of Lamentations.

If ever there was a book that began with immense suffering and dripped with grief in every word you read, this book is it.

During this time there was a brutal overthrow of Jerusalem by Nebuchadnezzar. It was incredibly dark circumstances for the people of Judah. They were in deep sorrow. They were grieving the loss of people, loss of their city, and loss of their temple. Pain flows in most words within Lamentations.

I was reading through this book wondering why God led me to read this particular instance in history. It was not only devastating, but emotionally draining to reflect over. Then I realized that the people of Jerusalem had created their own circumstances.

This was God's action because of the people of Judah's doing. Sin created the wreckage that the people of Judah were experiencing.

If we go back a few chapters in Ezekiel, we will find that the destruction they were about to experience was prophesied, because of their refusal to be obedient to the Lord.

When a man was chosen to become the prophet that would deliver words of the long-suffering ruin upon them, God told him this;

But the house of Israel will not want to listen to you because they do not want to listen to me. For the whole house of Israel is hardheaded and hardhearted. Look, I have made your face as hard as their faces and your forehead as hard as their foreheads. I have made your forehead like a diamond, harder than flint. Don't be afraid of them or discouraged by the look on their faces, though they are a rebellious house.

Ezekiel 3: 7-9

Rebellion.

In our humanness, we often rebel against what is of His Kingdom to attempt to fully utilize the worldly kingdom for our own gain, our own comfort, or our own pleasure. We are disobedient. We can create circumstances that bring us pain and we are the ones to be blamed. We can become stubborn in this and many times we refuse to acknowledge our own offenses.

That's hard to admit to, right?

When things happen in our life because of our sin. Because of our own doing. Because we made the choice.

I know, for myself, I do not like to sit in that. I don't like to admit to creating circumstances that are difficult to journey through.

The truth is that God is a jealous God. He is a God that does not enjoy watching His children create darkness within them and make wrong choices.

He parents us.

Parenting. If you've experienced a child in rebellion, you know that it can be insanely intense at times. My son went through a stage where he did not like to admit he was wrong. It was complete stubbornness. I would find myself gritting my teeth and struggling to force helpful words through my lips in times that I was overwhelmingly frustrated that he wouldn't just admit to his wrongdoings.

Sometimes these instances were accidental. Things happen. However, he would either deny he had done something wrong or refuse to even mutter an apology.

We would have to discipline him. We would have to redirect him. We would have to explain to him why what he did was selfish. Then it would hit me that I can do the exact same thing.

Sometimes out of stubbornness and selfish intent, I refuse to admit that I was in the wrong. I intentionally withhold apologies, because in my mind it makes me appear weak.

There have been many instances in my life where it was easier to deny my wrongdoings than to force feed myself the spoon of humbleness.

God allows me to decide. I get to make the decision if I will surrender up my desire for protecting my pride or if I will be humble in confessing to my own offenses.

We are granted the freedom of choice. We are free to make decisions in our life and sometimes we fail Him in our choices. Sometimes the choices we make aren't in alignment with His good and perfect will for our lives.

Therefore, we may endure times where we are disciplined because of circumstances that we've created ourselves.

The good news?

Jesus Christ.

God walked this Earth in human flesh and died for us. In the crucifixion of someone completely flawless, we are redeemed. He was the perfect man. Sinless. Our hands and feet should be on that cross, nailed in, hanging for our wrong doings but instead Jesus took our place.

For while we were still helpless, at the right time, Christ died for the ungodly. For rarely will someone die for a just person—though for a good person perhaps someone might even dare to die. But God proves his own love for us in that while we were still sinners, Christ died for us.

Romans 5:6-8

We can't defend our sin.

We can't justify our sin.

There is no, "But God, you don't understand..."

We must learn how to repent.

"Therefore, house of Israel, I will judge each one of you according to his ways. This is the declaration of the Lord God. Repent and turn away from all your rebellious acts, so they will not become a sinful stumbling block to you. Throw off the transgressions you have committed, and get yourselves a new heart and a new spirit. Why should you die, house of Israel? For I take no pleasure in anyone's death." This is the declaration of the Lord God, "So repent and live!" Ezekiel 18: 30-32

We must learn to have humility in order to admit to our wrongdoings and our shortcomings. We must admit to our disobedience and that we were living out of selfish intent. Sometimes we even must admit that the circumstances we are in, are not anyone else's doing, but circumstances we've created because of our own sin.

I had my family leave our community church.

I was incredibly ashamed to admit to that for a long time.

I allowed my pride to swallow me up and keep my family out of that body of community because of how a few people from it had treated me.

I was judged for what I did in my career, and if we are bluntly honest, I didn't want to continue supporting the church in any way because God had led me to the career I was in. I didn't want the subject myself any further to their judgment.

Pride darkens even the brightest hearts and creates fertile soil for bitterness to thrive.

Although judgment from others happened, it didn't mean I was being denied the opportunity to go forward in my God given callings. I was the one that allowed bitterness to blossom within my heart.

So there my young family was, floundering in a season of our life where we were not attending church.

We jumped around from church to church for a while, but the initial judgment and rejection continued to burn within me, never allowing us to find a place to call "home" in the church sense.

I could blame the church because it is easy to do, but the truth is I'm the one that shoulders the blame for the circumstances we found ourselves in.

Churches are full of broken people, not perfect ones.

When God said to go back because I would be needed, I resisted for as long as I could. The people who had judged me were still there. I had been unfriended on social media by some. I felt cast out, even if I was the one who refused to go. I felt like I was charging back in.

I was responsible for my own actions, not theirs.

To mutter the words, *this was my fault*, was hard to do. But I had to kill the garden of bitterness I had cultivated within my heart against the church.

You see, in Jerusalem, they admitted to their sin. They knew the destruction that fell upon them was their doing.

Because of the Lord's faithful love we do not perish, for his mercies never end. They are new every morning; great is your faithfulness!
Lamentations 3:22-23

Even during immense wreckage, the people of Judah were still crying out. They were not placing blame on the Lord, but instead they were offering up praise to Him.

What if we surrendered our pride for praise?

Our comfort was not secured on the cross, our freedom was. There isn't anything comfortable about the death of Christ, but there is immense glory worthy of our praise because of it.

What would happen if whatever circumstances we were in, we didn't have expectations of something that made us feel good? What if we met challenging circumstances with joy because we knew greatness would come because of it?

The discomfort of your flesh is temporary.

The promise of freedom is forever.

He is waiting for us to realize just how deeply loved we are by Him.

God does not withhold any good thing from you.

> *For the Lord God is a sun and shield. The Lord grants favor and honor; he does not withhold the good from those who live with integrity. Happy is the person who trusts in you, Lord of Armies!*
>
> *Psalms 84:11-12*

The good is there, but you must choose to receive it.

What the world says is good, is not always what is good for us. God's definition of good may be situations or circumstances that do not look good by the world.

There are many times in my life I've wondered why I had to trudge through difficult situations. How could there be good in that?

Let's go back to Rachel and Leah.

I think about Rachel's situation and how devastating her circumstances would have felt. There she was believing that Jacob would take her as his wife. The waiting was interrupted hugely by her father meddling and offering up Leah in Rachel's place. But Jacob fought for Rachel and ended up marrying her as well.

Then she finds out that she can't conceive, but her sister who stole her place was able to bear many children.

Her circumstances were obviously not ideal, and there was nothing about her sinful nature mentioned in creating these situations for her.

This story speaks on a deeper level, because circumstances designed by our own choices seems logical, but circumstances formed out of something beyond our understanding is difficult for us to not only comprehend but accept.

I know loved ones who have experienced extremely difficult circumstances that they can't fully comprehend, and they question why they are having to wade through those waters.

It isn't supposed to be this hard, right?

It isn't supposed to feel difficult when you've been faithful, right?

I don't have answers for the events that happen in our lives that feel catastrophic and unfair. Navigating the seasons of despair and destruction when you feel you've done nothing to deserve it, is more than the word "difficult" can encompass.

This I do know.

The Lord's ways are higher than ours.

For my thoughts are not your thoughts, and your ways are not my ways. This is the Lord's declaration. For as heaven is higher than earth, so my ways are higher than your ways, and my thoughts than your thoughts.
Isaiah 55:8-9

The truth is that we can plan for our life and we can live it with the best intentions, but that doesn't always mean that what we vision for ourselves ahead is what has been chartered for us.

The seasons and circumstances that we must navigate are not always going to be ones that we want to navigate through.

I lost a baby.

Miscarriage is difficult. My baby was around 7 weeks old when I discovered I was miscarrying.

I remember going to the hospital three days in a row to have my blood drawn to confirm that the baby was gone. My fair complexion caused the bruises from the needles to feel like they were neon-colored. I wore long sleeves to make sure no one saw the evidence.

At the time my oldest was a year old.

I didn't have a lot of mom connections to explain what was happening. I felt alone and defaulted to shame, which eventually became denial.

How could my body reject a sweet babe from entering our family?

Shortly after, I became pregnant again.

The quick rebound of a healthy pregnancy made me bury the hurt from losing a baby even deeper. I was thankful for new life but hadn't fully processed what had happened.

Then I began to feel guilty for the denial.

We can twist our emotions into all forms when we allow our circumstances to define them.

Our circumstances do not define us.

I don't know why I lost a baby, but I trust that the One who holds the entire world can hold any moment in my life.

When you are feeling shame or guilt, do not hide yourself from the world. We can tend to withdraw from others when we feel broken.

You don't need to filter your life to make it good.

Trust in the Lord with all your heart, and do not rely on your own understanding; in all your ways know him, and he will make your paths straight. Proverbs 3: 5-6

You can lean into the Lord who knows you fully and give Him your complete trust in all circumstances. You don't have to understand everything; you just need to know God. When we lean into Him, He guides our footsteps forward.

In all seasons, God gently breathes purpose into them. We may not always comprehend the purpose and the purpose may be for a larger gain than only for ourselves.

Have you ever looked at your seasons and circumstances in that way?

Your life story is to be used for a bigger purpose than your own benefit.

Your life intertwines with a salvation purpose to restore His glory among His people. Your life, in every season, is carefully being woven into a story that can resonate with the lost, so they can shout out to be found. Your seasons matter.

Your seasons of wait.

Your seasons of rest.

Your seasons of charging forward.

Your seasons of feeling lost.

Your seasons of being found.

How can God rise up His people, if they only experience seasons of precise direction?

There is mighty purpose in seasons of more difficult circumstances in order to reach those who desperately need to see that redemption isn't reserved for a certain few.

He isn't just preparing you to rise up in your seasons, He is preparing the rising up of His people. He is preparing the next generation who will testify to His goodness in all circumstances.

It's a little hard to accomplish the task of reviving His Kingdom when there are no people who can create a revival out of their own brokenness.

Seasons are necessary. Circumstances are necessary.

You must recognize them for what they truly are, chapters of a bigger story written to glorify Him.

There is an occasion for everything, and a time for every activity under heaven: a time to give birth and a time to die; a time to plant and a time to uproot; a time to kill and a time to heal; a time to tear down and a time to build; a time to weep and a time to laugh; a time to mourn and a time to dance; a time to throw stones and a time to gather stones; a time to embrace and a time to avoid embracing; a time to search and a time to count as lost; a time to keep and a time to throw away; a time to tear and a time to sew; a time to be silent and a time to speak; a time to love and a time to hate; a time for war and a time for peace.

Ecclesiastes 3: 1-8

Time is fleeting and embracing our seasons is necessary in order to learn how God is working within us, so we understand what He is creating through us.

If people oversaw choosing their seasons, they would only choose the ones that made life feel easy. Our human nature desires for comfort and pleasure. In the verses above, we would easily choose healing, building, laughing, dancing and loving.

However, if we made the choice to miss the seasons of restlessness, mourning, feeling torn down and waiting, we would rob ourselves of how those seasons prepare us for immense growth in Christ. This is where we press in and realize the desperate longing we have for Jesus.

Time is a gift from God. Time is our opportunity to embrace in all seasons. We cannot waste away our time by desiring new seasons.

I recently entered a new season of motherhood. For eight years, my home was full of laughter, tears, tantrums, noise, hours of snuggles, and having a little person constantly clinging to my side.

During the seasons of early motherhood, there were many times I longed for a new season. The season where I got to enjoy some alone time and could process thoughts in my own head. I wanted more than spit up on my t-shirt and dry shampoo in my hair. I felt overwhelmed and desired peace within my chaos.

If I could go back, I would tell that younger version of myself that there was peace available in that chaos all along. I was the one choosing not to embrace the season I was in, because it was hard and all consuming. My season of young motherhood was necessary, and it was purposeful in its' own unique way.

Now, my new season of motherhood encompasses hours of quiet. I find myself longing for school pick-up when I can once again feel filled up by their rambunctious joy within the walls of my home.

But I cannot place my focus on what was or what will come, but what is in the right now.

My new season allows for me to take those thoughts that once raced through my head and complete them so I can write to fulfill a new calling in a new season.

Seasons, even when they feel long, are truly fleeting. Time is sacred and so many times we waste it wishing for different circumstances.

The seasons and circumstances you are experiencing now are important. We were created for more than a single moment in time, a single occurrence, a single victory. We were created for an eternal life.

When we can truly focus on the steadfastness that is God, we can better navigate the seasons we must go through that are always changing. Our God never changes. He is our constant. He is our compass. He is our due North.

When we look to Him and choose to steer through our seasons with the assurance that God is leading us into an abundant life with Him, we can feel a peace in our circumstances even when they feel challenging or chaotic.

There is a bigger story being written than what you are experiencing in the right now.

What does the worker gain from his struggles? I have seen the task that God has given the children of Adam to keep them occupied. He has made everything appropriate in its time. He has also put eternity in their hearts, but no one can discover the work God has done from beginning to end. I know that there is nothing better for them than to rejoice and enjoy the good life. It is also the gift of God whenever anyone eats, drinks and enjoys all his efforts. I know that everything God does will last forever; there is no adding to it or taking from it. God works so that people will be in awe of him. Whatever is, has already been, and whatever will be, already is. However, God seeks justice for the persecuted.

Ecclesiastes 3:9-15

The good life.

Friend, the good life is life right now.

The good life doesn't mean lush surroundings, popular status, or worldly splendor. The good life doesn't mean being comfortable, feeling at ease, or checking off accomplishments. The good life doesn't look like the perfection you see in your newsfeeds.

The good life isn't attached to your circumstances. The good life is the one that embraces and rejoices in the current season.

The good life is attached to the fact that you are redeemed.

The good life is one that recognizes your true freedom was acquired through the sacrifice of Jesus Christ.

God's plans are eternal plans. They are beyond worldly understanding and standards. We were destined for more than this world can offer and more than it is able to comprehend.

Seasons are a test to our character.

Our seasons have the ability to mold us into the person God needs us to become for His Kingdom.

If we were able to walk through life with ease, would we cry out for the strength of our Savior?

If we never experienced struggle, would we delight in all victories, big and small, in our life?

If we didn't understand the desire for redemption in our life, would we choose to look to Him for guidance?

It is okay to wade through deep waters and it's okay to splash around in shallow pools. The tides of your life will constantly fluctuate.

You cannot continue to compare your seasons or your circumstances with others. Your social media feed is not a place to go for guidance on what your life should look like right now.

God doesn't compare seasons to seasons, or circumstances to circumstances. He intentionally guides us to grow us. He creates opportunity for us to surrender to Him to strengthen us.

You are needed in your current season.

Don't lose sight on the bigger picture and don't miss out on the beauty that is your season right now.

You are a seed pushing through the dirt, looking for the breath of fresh air and the rush of blooming in the sunshine. You can't become that flower without the experience of feeling lost or forgotten among the dark soil and taking root into the Giver of life itself.

There is intricate purpose in what happens before a seed can sprout in renewed strength. Be refreshed by His outpouring of grace extended to you through His mighty love for you. He loves you when you are a small seed navigating to the surface and when you are a flower blooming in the sunshine. The process is what created the flower and it was intricately designed.

It's beautiful we are given the opportunity to live a life navigating through changing seasons and circumstances. It's wonderful we are given grace when we choose to steer in our own direction instead of His own. It's fortunate we get to experience life here on earth in a way that allows us to embrace a journey to eternal life, instead of one that fades with the changing of time.

Our reward for being obedient and relying on His steadfast love through all seasons, is walking through the majestically adorned gates of heaven where the joy we were able to grasp in all circumstances of our life, is magnified beyond our understanding.

Be present in your seasons and be grateful towards them, because they are part of a larger process in your purpose than you can even imagine.

-8-

STEPPING FORWARD IN BOLDNESS

Life is not easy is a phrase that I usually respond to with an eye roll, even though I've muttered it multiple times to my children and my friends.

I heard this phrase many times growing up and even though it may be an overused statement, it is valid and true. Life wasn't meant to be easy. Hardships are meant to strengthen us and allow us to become a greater version of ourselves. You may catch glimmers of comfort, but the secret to living a life of full purpose is becoming well-known with the uncomfortable. The uncomfortable is where we are going to find the soil to root down and flourish within His Kingdom. Growth happens in the uncomfortable.

People tend to steer clear of the uncomfortable. No one likes to put themselves in uneasy situations. Take a rose for instance—I love the flower itself, not the thorns.

Enamored by the beauty of the vibrant petals, people want to clip off the thorns to make the beauty comfortable. No one likes to hold a rose that causes them pain. However, that rose grew from the thorns. The thorns are symbols of hardiness and they protected the rose from harm.

We are like a rose.

Our thorns are symbols of hardships that we have chosen to wear on the outside, instead of internalizing them, which enables God's strength to be seen through our weakness. When we allow the uncomfortable to be seen, we are also allowing God to protect us in our vulnerability. Throughout this entire uncomfortable process, we are allowed the opportunity to bloom most beautifully as the rose with the vibrant petals.

You see, God doesn't want us hidden. He doesn't want us to not be seen. He wants us to be seen in the way He sees us, in His marvelous light. He wants the world to see our beauty as much as they have seen our struggles.

There is this concept in our world that tells us as women of Christ, that our beauty and our strengths need to be watered down and made comfortable for others. We can share in our weaknesses if we don't over share in our goodness. We should present ourselves as less than so that others feel more comfortable accepting us.

People are okay with seeing our thorns, but they are not always okay with seeing our vibrant petals.

If we show up as a secure and confident woman, we may intimidate others. Instead, we are supposed to "tone it down" so that we don't make anyone feel threatened.

If we find ourselves blooming before someone else does, we may make them feel inferior. Instead, we should stunt our growth to make it more comfortable for the women around us.

I took my kids to the park one day and ended up with my oldest daughter sobbing on my lap for thirty minutes.

Her siblings didn't like the game she wanted to play and they had decided to play a game of their own.

I held her and tried to reason with her—realizing that I was also giving myself a pep talk. That very week I had been rejected by someone I had once thought as a friend.

I told my daughter that just because her brother and sister didn't think her game sounded fun, it didn't mean that it wasn't fun. The game she wanted to play wasn't a lesser option. I encouraged her that she could continue playing her own game if that is what she wanted to do, and someone may eventually join her.

What we bring to the table isn't "less than" because not everyone wants to join in. What we can provide in our passions, our gifts and our ideas aren't less worthy of being seen and heard because others don't understand it or simply don't like it. There will be some that truly see you and think the things you are doing in your life are absolutely amazing. They see you rising up to your God given potential and they may even want to join in with you.

There will be people who love you and people who don't. It's okay.

We don't have to take the opinions of others as truth, because the opinions of others will never be enough anyway. We can continue to play the game we were suited up for even if it isn't the same game as the others around us.

At the end of the day, I truly believe that each of us do not want to drop to our knees and apologize to God for not showing up in the way He asked us to, because we were afraid of what other people would think of us.

We need to stop watering ourselves down, because we are simply keeping ourselves from rising up to the version that God intended for each of us to become.

God did not create you and save you to be less than you are. He did not call you to dim your light, He called you to shine it. He called you to set the world ablaze with His majestic fire. You are doing God a disservice when you show up as less than. You must be able to dig down deep and find the confidence that God has given you to be more.

This is contradictory to many things you hear in our society today.

Be more.

We are told *you are enough*.

We are told to *be content*.

Although these phrases when paired with biblical truths can hold importance, they fall short when we decide we are enough and can be content within worldly standards.

Haven't I commanded you: be strong and courageous? Do not be afraid or discouraged, for the Lord your God is with you wherever you go.
Joshua 1:9

We don't need to fear the rejection of other women when we show up boldly in Whose we were created. The entire purpose of the idea of not intimidating other women is to create a fear among us. A fear to divide us.

When we continue showing up as less than in order to present ourselves as relatable and acceptable to others, it keeps the Kingdom of God from rising up.

When we are not presenting ourselves boldly as the truest version of ourselves in who God created within us, our gifts are not seen and are less likely to be used.

We become a watered-down community that douses the fire of God.

We try so hard to be relatable with one another.

However, we aren't called to relate. We are called to set others free.

We need to replace the word *relate* with *relevant*.

The world needs to experience relevant women who are showing up with applicable ideas for others to implement in their daily lives to grow, instead of remaining stagnant in their watered-down lives.

Being relevant allows us the opportunity to present our growing relationship with Jesus Christ. It extends the invitation to others who want to dive deeper into their own growth and become more in Him.

When we relate with someone, it can speak this unsaid permission that they don't need to dive deeper and press forward more boldly.

When we are relevant with someone, it shows others that they can be different and changed for His good.

The church needs women to come together boldly showing up in all their unique gifts. When we can "community" together with the spirit of success in Christ, instead of the success in ourselves, our eyes will be opened to how everyone can be used differently but with the same purpose.

Rise up women with boldness and confidence in Christ. We are hungry for more because we were created for more. Do not buy into the lies that the world throws at you in order to feel better about yourself. Do not buy into the lies so you feel accepted by others. It is temporary. The world doesn't want us to become more in Christ.

Do you know what happens when you step up and become more in Christ?

You have people who are secure in Christ and absolutely understand that their very best is what Christ has intended for them.

They don't look down as they take bold step after bold step chasing down what they were made for. They become fearless because of the power graciously given by God within them. Doubts and worries vanish from their mind because they know they are simply distractions from stepping into the position they have been given.

Friend, I just described a soldier suited up for battle.

We must move forward. We must put blinders on, look ahead, and do the things we are called to do with conviction even when we are battling the nervous butterflies.

We should not be okay with being complacent.

The definition of complacent means to be calm and secure in oneself. Initially this sounds pretty good. I know I have desired to be calm and secure in myself. However, there is a difference between being secure in oneself and being secured in the name of Christ.

Coming from a place of complacence breeds pride, self-satisfaction, self-importance, and a life that becomes unaware to actual dangers or deficiencies.

Plain and simple; it's ignorance.

If we become complacent, how easy would it be for the devil to come and destroy? Those wrapped up in complacency are unaware of the dangers that the devil is plotting.

Complacency allows us to become lukewarm.

I know your works, that you are neither cold nor hot. I wish that you were cold or hot. So, because you are lukewarm, and neither hot nor cold, I am going to vomit you out of my mouth. Revelation 3:15-16

Being lukewarm signifies a lack of commitment to the Lord. It is an attitude or way of life, where someone claims to know God, but they live their life as if He doesn't exist.

The devil fishes from a lukewarm pond. Don't let him bait you.

You must turn up the heat.

You were made for more and you were made to passionately pursue purpose that burns within your body and that boldly shines the love of Christ.

Don't think you aren't capable, friend. The hands that molded you are the most powerful. They shaped you and created you. Don't allow the world to rob you of that power that flows within your veins.

God sees you and He wants you to be seen because His light will radiate brilliantly to those around you.

When you weaken yourself, you fade to a less vibrant version of who you were created to be. You aren't enough without Him, friend. I say that with so much love but also with a pressing urgency for you to see yourself as a woman who can overcome and overtake the fears in your life, to be more than you are right now.

The fears that tell you, you aren't worthy of being more.

The fears that tell you, you don't have the capability of becoming more.

The fears that tell you, you simply aren't enough to do more.

The fears that tell you about the responsibility that will come, when you do become more.

Are you scared of becoming more than you are?

Fear is actually fearful of our own potential.

Fear wants to cut us down before we can grow into more.

Fear will feed you spoonful after spoonful of lies all day long, because fear knows it can destroy you with the ammo it possesses. The devil preys on your weakness. However, when you package up that weakness and hand it over to the one true God who is more powerful than yourself, fear trembles.

Friend, you have power.

There is ultimate power running through your veins when you allow God to fill you up as the vessel you were created to become for Him. He wants to fill you up with capability, with love, with strength, with so much more than you can even imagine.

You are strong. You are brave and you are so, incredibly capable of being bold and showing up as more, because you have been called to become more.

Some days it is hard to show up in that power.

Some days it is difficult to step forward in what God is calling us to pursue.

Some days the load seems to heavy to bear.

Jesus asked for His load to be lightened.

He went out and made his way as usual to the Mount of Olives, and the disciples followed him. When he reached the place, he told them, "Pray that you may not fall into temptation." Then he withdrew from them about a stone's throw, knelt down, and began to pray, "Father, if you are willing, take this cup away from me—nevertheless, not my will, but yours, be done." Luke 22:39-42

When it feels hard to press forward boldly, know Jesus asked for His cup to be taken from Him too.

We aren't weak when we ask for the harder things in our life to be taken from us.

Jesus sat where you sat.

Jesus knew the hard things that were coming against Him.

But He knew God's will would be done.

Then an angel from heaven appeared to him, strengthening him. Luke 22:43

You are not alone.

God secures your steps forward when done out of obedience.

With our social media presence, we can tend to tone down our boldness so others will receive us well.

We are intimidated by the thought of what being bold will do to our image.

It can cause people to hit that "unfriend" button or comment unkindly.

Being bold in our world of social media is an open invitation to allow conflict. People seem to forget that a person with a real, beating heart exists behind the screen.

It's been a battle to learn to detach my emotions from worldly agendas on social media.

There is almost nothing in this world that I try to avoid more than confrontation.

Confrontation makes me grind my teeth and my stomach swirl. I cringe at the idea of having to hash out ideologies or beliefs with anyone else. It is more comfortable to sit in a bubble of protection and guard my social media from the possibility of trolls that have an agenda to take me down for their own pleasure.

I was once sent a nasty message on Facebook.

Okay, maybe more than once, but this particular conversation ended up in this woman not only unfriending me but blocking me too.

The worst part?

It was over a post that I had created to *encourage* mothers in their daily undertakings—whether they were stay at home moms, work from home moms or working moms. No matter how we are called to mother, it's all hard work.

I'm not even sure what part it was that caused her to have an agenda against me, but it ended with her lashing out in a very ugly way in a personal Facebook message.

I remember receiving the message and my heart stopped. I'm pretty sure that is what happened. Confrontation makes me lose my pulse. Until it suddenly jump-started like a car coming back to life after it died. My initial reaction was being dumbfounded and a little more than slightly irritated with the incredibly, incorrect assumptions she had made about me.

What caused her to believe that she could send me a message shaming me for my own encouraging post on my own page?

I wasn't even saying anything that held the power to ruffle feathers, or so I thought. What would have happened if I would have said something more boldly?

I calmly replied after several deep breaths. I even sent her another encouraging message, because that is what I do. I don't wish to use my tongue like a sword even if we have been trained to be defensive in our responses to conflict.

I received one last very blunt, arrogant message where she called me many offensive names and then suddenly, I was blocked.

Out of all of that, here is my point—I only knew this person through Facebook and unless she had been very closely following me, she really did not know me. When I unknowingly stepped on her toes, she did not take it lightly.

She could have chosen to scroll on by since we really aren't friends.

She could have muttered to herself and then got over it.

But that is not what happened.

She took it personally even when it wasn't intended to be personal, and she decided to send me a nasty message all because she had the inability to swallow her judgement of other people, and be okay with thinking differently.

These types of interactions cause us to shrink back.

No one likes to receive messages in their inbox that are only meant to shame them or shake them up with frustration or anger. No one likes to be judged for any part of who they are, including their opinions and their choices.

As a society we have become quick to judge and even quicker to tear other people down.

The thought of being bold is something we should pause on, but it shouldn't cause us not to act either.

Wise people think before they act; fools don't---and even brag about their foolishness. Proverbs 13:16

We need to be wise in our responses. We need to become well practiced in our boldness so that when a foolish person decides to attack, we are easily equipped with the ability to continue to stand up and not shrink back.

Boldness is stepping into your greatness. It is the act of being confident in who God intended you to be. You do not doubt because you have intently listened to your Father who has prepared the journey ahead for you. Instead of being insecure in the message you have to deliver and the journey you've been called to walk, you become filled with a desire to share with the world the freeness that God has given you to walk forward boldly.

We should never feel like we must water ourselves down to be accepted by the people of this world. We are not looking for acceptance from people.

For what will it benefit someone if he gains the whole world yet loses his life? Or what will anyone give in exchange for his life? For the Son of Man is going to come with his angels in the glory of his Father, and then he will reward each according to what he has done. Matthew 16:26-27

Obedience is at the core of the work we've been given. We aren't here to impress the world. We are here to press boldly into the love of Christ and then shower the world with that bold love. Bold love equates to stepping into the greatness of who God created you to become. You were created in love. You can boldly love others, even when it isn't comfortable.

Your light is needed. You do not need to dim your light when it makes others uncomfortable. You cannot allow the insecurities of others to keep you from sharing the message God has given you to share.

If others complain when you fully accept who you are because of Whose you are, they can simply step aside.

Don't allow their ignorance to create insecurity within you. You were given incredible purpose before anyone ever had an opinion about you. You were created for more.

We planted trees on Good Friday this last year.

It made me wonder—Did the tree that grew from its' little seed, know it was going to be used as the board Jesus Christ would hang upon?

As the tree was cut and prepared, did it know its' role in the Kingdom redemption story?

As Christ drug it through the streets with the heaviness of the world's sins on His shoulders, did the

As Christ drug it through the streets with the heaviness of the worlds' sins on His shoulders, did the tree feel the strength of Jesus?

As Christ hung heavy on what was once branches, did the tree feel the weight of our own brokenness Jesus was carrying?

As Christ's blood stained the wood, did the tree know the redeeming power that was seeping within it?

As Christ drew His last breath and the Earth and Heavens wept, did the tree feel the magnitude of the moment?

The tree's purpose from the very beginning of its' life was larger than it ever planned.

We don't know what our complete redemption story looks like, but we know who our Redeemer is.

When you've felt cut down and made into something different than you thought you were made for, open your eyes to the bigger picture.

You were made to display redemption, just as that tree will forever be entwined in the Easter story of glory.

You were made to shout, "He is Risen!", because with His rising He lifted your sins.

You were made for great purpose, because God knows you intimately as your Creator and sent His **only Son** to die for you.

The tree may have felt the heaviness of the weight of Christ's death, but the tree also felt the weight lifted through His redemptive death.

You don't have to carry your shame, your sin, or your guilt—Jesus already paid the price.

Become a vessel of His glory and move forwardly boldly knowing His plans for you are significant.

You were created for more than the mediocrity of a worldly life. You were created for life eternal.

Press forward friend. Your boldness is needed.

-9-

YOU ARE KNOWN

Before this conversation comes to an end, I wanted to warn you that there will be temptations. You may feel equipped and prepared for the days to come, absorbing in the truth of Whose you are instead of attempting to gain worldly praise but remember—there are days coming that you will need to stop, breathe deeply, and refill yourself with God's strength.

Temptations from the world will continue to distract us from our eternal purpose. Those temptations cause us to look away instead of looking up to Him. Temptations are stumbling blocks and in a world of social media, you are going to experience them often.

I was lost searching for something more than myself for a very long time. When I thought I had grasped onto something, I didn't recognize that while I was in awe soaking in what the world was offering me, the world was silently slipping on shackles.

I was able to shake those shackles off because I found freedom in Whose I am in my Father. God had been offering me true freedom all along.

My tunnel focus on promised worldly things seemed magnificent at the time.

But it was based on workings from my human flesh.

I had to sacrifice things that were important to me. I had to be in a constant hustle to stay within the focus of other people for recognition, for acceptance, for validation, for love, or for some sort of achievement status to make me appear to be worthy and capable.

It was absolutely all consuming, completely exhausting, and robbed me of any peace.

I was never fulfilled.

Once I stopped hustling for myself and surrendered my pride and shame at His feet, others saw my disposition change.

I lost the attention of some people.

There would be opportunities for me to seek their approval and it would look incredibly tempting. There would be times their praise flattered someone else and I had to calm the prideful voice within myself that wanted it to be me. My selfish tendencies would crop up and I would want to be the one in their spotlight.

Temptations to become known, to feel loved, and to receive validation in a worldly sense will continually come up in your life and you will have to battle it, friend.

A Godly ordained life cannot coexist with worldly striving.

There is emptiness in pleasure. There is emptiness in possessions. There is emptiness in status. There is emptiness in the worldly search.

Even though there is emptiness, it can appear to be full.

I had a cup as a kid that I absolutely loved. It had colored liquid on the outside of the cup so that it always appeared to have something in it. It moved like water and it appeared to be full, but it was an illusion.

That is how the worldly cup appears. It's an illusion that allows you to believe that what you are focused on is something full of goodness that will refresh your soul and your life.

However, once you obtain the cup, you realize that it's dry within.

The well of the world is dry and it will never be able to quench your desires, but the well of the Kingdom is overflowing with Living Water.

We are tempted by the empty cup, often wanting to believe that there truly is something inside it.

Temptation is guaranteed in a world where the devil resides.

Then Jesus was led up by the Spirit into the wilderness to be tempted by the devil. After he had fasted forty days and forty nights, he was hungry.
Matthew 4:1-2

Jesus was tempted.

He had created a physical hunger within himself and the devil saw it. The devil offered up all he could from the resources of the world.

Again, the devil took him to a very high mountain and showed him all the kingdoms of the world and their splendor. And he said to him, "I will give you all these things if you fall down and worship me."

Matthew 4:8-9

But Jesus did not take from the Devil's empty cup. He knew, even in His discomfort from wandering the wilderness for many days, that what the Devil offered up of the world was not worth sacrificing His Father's eternal promises.

What the world gives, even in all its' splendor, looks like a flame of a candle being compared to the brightness of the sun.

Satan likes to parade us through the success, pleasures, desires, and splendors of the world. He likes to show them off to us in order to persuade us that we can somehow push through and earn those worldly things.

The temptations you are up against can better be handled when you fully immerse yourself in the gracious love of God. You get to decide to accept what He has to offer you over what the world is tempting you with. You can surrender over control of your life to Someone who is better matched to handle what you are up against in the world's temptation game.

We are either working on our relationship with God or working on our relationship with the world. The people in the world needs Jesus. They're in desperate desire of Jesus. The bold way of life is choosing your relationship with God over your relationship with the world and its' ways. This can bring on rejection and disappointment from other people who are pressing different demands from you. However, the good news is in doing this, you are becoming a beacon of hope for the people who are currently lost in the empty promises of the world—who have taken from the empty cup.

Playing it safe in this world or choosing worldly striving will end in eventual regret if you compromised your relationship with your Maker for trophies and possessions that will fade into dust in the end.

I do not want to trade my soul for the fading glory of a useless trophy.

Do you?

Let's take the people of Jerusalem once again. They were exiled for 70 years. God left the city. He **left** them. I get shivers in how that must have felt as it rippled over the city. Certainly, a chill coated their bodies as they felt the warmth of the love and presence of their Father leave. He left because they had refused to listen to Him. Instead they decided to succumb to the whispers of lies the world was telling them.

God returned, but there was still struggle.

When it was time for Jerusalem to be rebuilt, they continued to suffer under their own work.

Now the Lord of Armies says this: "Think carefully about your ways. You have planted much but harvested little. You eat but never have enough to be satisfied. You drink but never have enough to be happy. You put on clothes but never have enough to get warm. The wage earner puts his wages into a bag with a hole in it." Haggai 1:5-6

They had built their houses before they built the Lord's house and they were struggling in their striving.

My husband and I are on a journey of building our home. We were able to purchase the land we wanted, we have the house plan picked out, dreams of what it will look like inside, visions of the garden, the sunflower patch, and more. We have carefully and creatively given vision for this beautiful home that our family will grow up in for many years to come.

When we went to apply for a loan the first time, we were turned down.

That was a difficult "no" to process. I struggled with it because I had been telling myself that we were being blessed by God in our finances and we would soon be building this gorgeous home. I had become so attached to the vision, that I had left out so many leading parts up to the actual breaking of ground of our own home.

I wanted to argue. To be told we were not financially stable enough for a loan for this home we were envisioning was a gut punch. My stubbornness wanted to continue the pursuit. I wanted to discover a loophole or continue seeking out banks until someone would finally decide to take a chance on us.

But that's the factor that was the main issue.

Take a chance *on us.*

If I was desiring for someone to take a chance on us, where was my faith in the Lord?

It wasn't our time for our home to be built and He had gently sent His "no" in the form of not being approved for the financial backing to begin the project.

There was a great temptation that cropped up in me to begin chasing worldly things so I could acquire the worldly things I desired.

It wasn't until a few months later that I began to realize this loud connection to our circumstances. It was so evident when I thought of it, that I wondered why it had taken me weeks to see the correlation.

It wasn't our time because it was His time for me to concentrate on building up His Kingdom, of investing my time and energy into not just my relationship with Him but into learning to put my worldly desires down to pick up the desires He had crafted specifically for my heart to build up His house.

Unless the Lord builds a house, its builders labor over it in vain.

Psalms 127: 1a

I needed to quiet my pride, follow His promptings to build His Kingdom in the way I was created to do, and when His timing for the building of our house arrived, it would not be done in vain but instead in peace.

The disapproval of the loan came 3 months before I began writing this book. It came 2 months before I began to feel the shedding of my worldly desires and the desire to clothe myself in His bold and beautiful truths for myself and my life.

You have a purpose, friend.

A deep, incredibly important purpose and He is waiting for you to boldly step into the laboring position that He has bestowed upon your life for His house in the form of your callings. He wants you to create the home for His Kingdom to be revived, to be renewed, and to rest in His love and promises.

You are the house. When you boldly choose to build yourself up in Him, you build up His Kingdom. You lay down the worldly kingdom desires that may have created excitement but eventual emptiness in your life.

This isn't easy to do. In fact, it is counter cultural.

You did not choose me, but I chose you. I appointed you to go and produce fruit and that your fruit should remain, so that whatever you ask the Father in my name, he will give you. John 15:16

You are chosen and you are chosen to produce fruit. His fruit. Fruit that provides everlasting life through choosing to build up His name over yours.

Not fame. Not fortune.

This is your time. Your time to step into the greatness that has been planned for you. Not greatness laid out by this world, but greatness that was instilled within you by your Creator.

The world needs you to show up. You do not need the world to show up for you.

When you can stop worrying about what the world thinks of you and instead fully encompass the fact that the opinion of only One matters, you can drop this idea of being validated and recognized by people of the world.

Their validation does not matter.

You need to wake up in the morning and not search for a solution in your life but wake up confidently understanding that you are the solution created by God who saw you as His success long before you recognized it. When you rise up and realize that you were created with a deep purpose and incredible gifts that can be utilized for His Kingdom, can you even imagine the proud smile God is displaying? He is your Father and He cares about you on such an intimate level that us, as mere humans, can only faintly recognize it. It's supernatural, beyond the capacity of understanding in this world we live in.

It's your time to rise up, to own up to the purpose you feel pulsing through your veins that has laid dormant for entirely too long. The world needs you to show up because you were made for something spectacular to change it, to inspire it on a Kingdom level.

Your purpose may not come with any fancy titles or recognition or applause from the people of this world. I want you to soak that in for a minute because there will be those that do rise up in this world with fancy titles and recognition. There will be those that receive the applause of people.

There is a difference between those who were seeking that applause and those who gained it as a side effect of chasing their callings given to them by God.

But remember this, their calling is not more important than your own. It is simply different. God couldn't make all of us the same.

How boring would all our stories read if we all were created equally in all things?

We were all created exclusively and matchless, which means that we cannot compare ourselves to one another. We are each rare. Irreplaceable.

So, if you compare yourself to someone else, you are simply wasting your time. Precious time that you could be spending on the things God wants you to do.

You'll watch some grow in their social media presence. They'll gain followers. They'll receive more likes. They'll be recognized and applauded.

This does not take away from you.

Their success is not your failure.

I want you to imagine posting something on your social media account. It's solid. Transparent. Bold. It's radiates the uniqueness that God created within you.

No one shows up.

No likes.

No comments.

Now I'm asking you, if you made a post that you felt held impact and it went unnoticed, will you be okay?

Will the fact that no one is acknowledging that they see you, cause you discomfort? Will it cause you to become emotionally distraught?

You need to be able to get to the point that you will be okay.

You see, when you decide that you are done with validation of the world and you only need the validation of God, a post with no reactions isn't something that should shake you.

You aren't here to impress people. You are here to make an impression on people in a special way only you were created to do.

God saw a need in this world. While He was creating you, He envisioned carefully what this world would need in order to see His love and His grace. Then, he delicately and purposefully placed unique giftings, specific traits, and burning passions within you to be the person He needed to show up.

The world is waiting. God is waiting.

He's waiting for you to shed the shame, the fear, the unknowns, the righteousness, the doubts, the lies, the need for approval, the desire for seeing your name in lights, the love of knowing you are seen by others...

He's waiting for you to die to yourself because He sent His son to die for you.

Don't allow the world to swallow you up. Don't allow Satan to snuff out that light that burns within you. Don't allow people to dictate who you can be.

Your Father in Heaven has already spoken the truth of who you are. He has validated your purpose. He has recognized your potential.

There is no need to ask the world for anything when you have already received it all. You just haven't opened your arms fully.

Friend, you are equipped.

With a solid foundation that you firmly plant your feet upon, you can withstand the workings of this world that are meant to work you over. You can not only shine His light, but you are able to hike up the tallest mountain, amp up that Light, and let the world see Him. What burns within you has nothing to do with your own glory or fame.

You are seen clearly.

You are loved deeply.

You are exclusive.

You are molded uniquely.

You are known fully, intimately, and accepted for it.

You are not on your own. God's walking beside you. He's right there. You can reach out to Him and He will hold your hand.

This world only seems scary because we make it seem that way. It's actually exciting. It's full of possibilities for you to step into it, shake it up, impact it, and shine Light so darkness cannot hide itself any longer.

Don't steer yourself any direction you choose. Cry out to the Master Navigator who has already walked the path in front of you.

I took a trip with friends once to Branson, Missouri. I rode in the back of the van and it would have been fine except for my motion sickness. During the day when we were weaving in and out of the hills, I would become sick, but at night I was laughing in the backseat having an amazing time on the ride.

During the day I had the opportunity to see the road ahead of me. I saw the twists and turns, the ups and downs. I saw what was coming and my body responded in a way that was full of uneasiness.

When we took the same twists and turns, ups and downs in the darkness where only the headlights illuminated a small part of the journey, my mind couldn't tell my body about the nervousness of what it saw further ahead.

We aren't meant to know the journey ahead of us. We aren't meant to see the twists and the turns or the ups and downs. If we did, we may not decide to take the road, but instead find an easier path that doesn't yield the same destination. Or we may just pull over and decide to be okay with where we are at.

God lights up only what we need to see. He does that for purpose. He may give us glimpses of our future destination, but He wants us to have faith that He will safely navigate us up and down those hills and around those twists and turns.

Your word is a lamp to my feet and a light to my path. Psalm 119:105

He gives us enough light and He gives us the best resource to keep us on our path without knowing the entire journey ahead—His Word. He needs us dependent on Him in order to fulfill His purpose in our life so that we don't decide to pave our own paths or run ahead of Him in our journey.

His timing is perfect timing. His path is the perfect path, potholes and all.

Just as I was laughing and enjoying my time in the dark driving through the hills of Missouri, He wants you to be able to put your full trust in Him and delight in the journey He has given you, even if it isn't what you expected. Even if you must go down a deep valley. Even if you struggle climbing up a mountain. Even if you find yourself with a flat tire on the side of the road.

You were made for purpose dear friend, and He will see it through to the end if you will decide to be okay with the simple light right in front of you and an unknown journey to embark on.

You don't need to know the details. Your God knows the details.

"For I know the plans I have for you"---this is the Lord's declaration—plans for your well-being, not for disaster, to give you a future and a

hope. You will call to me and come and pray to me, and I will listen to you. You will seek me and find me when you search for me with all your heart. I will be found by you". Jeremiah 29:11-14a

His plans are for your good. If you scrap them and decide your own plans are better, you'll never know the amazing goodness He has planned out for you. If you've made plans for yourself and already went through with them, read the verse above again because we serve a God of restoration. Even when our hearts rebels repeatedly, God promises to restore us. He does not abandon His children. He will never abandon you. He continues to chase you down and fight for you until you are found.

You, friend, are incredibly pursued by a Father of compassion and mercy.

Have faith that who you are because of Whose you are is more than enough.

Have faith that being known by your Father in Heaven is worth a million times over being known by millions of people.

Have faith that the giftings and the traits He has placed within you are glorious and needed.

Have faith, friend, that it's your time to stand up, be bold, and journey the path God has destined for you. Just you.

How incredibly special is that? An entire life planned out specifically for you. You can't tell me that you aren't important when the God of all things laid a path down for you brick-by-brick for you to walk down. It's your red carpet. It's your yellow brick road. It's uniquely yours.

I will give you thanks with all my heart; I will sing your praise before the heavenly beings. I will bow down toward your holy temple and give thanks to your name for your constant love and truth. You have exalted your name and your promise above everything else. On the day I called, you answered me; you increased strength within me.

All the kings on earth will give you thanks, Lord, when they hear what you have promised. They will sing of the Lord's ways, for the Lord's glory is great. Though the Lord is exalted, he takes note of the humble; but he knows the haughty from a distance.

If I walk into the thick of danger, you will preserve my life from the anger of my enemies. You will extend your hand; your right hand will save me. The Lord will fulfill his purpose for me. Lord, your faithful love endures forever; do not abandon the work of your hands.

Psalms 138: 1-8

Allow gratitude to spill out from your very being. Allow joy to bubble up in all circumstances and praise your Father in Heaven who has continued to love you through it all.

He will continue to seek you until you realize that you have been fully known all along on your journey of seeking worldly approval.

You are allowed to love the life you have been given. You are allowed to do amazing things. You are allowed to step into the greatness planned out for you that allows God to be glorified.

Let's be confident women radiating the beauty and power He has crafted within each of us. Let's come together and boldly lift high the Kingdom of God through one another because we know that our differences are an edge to our battle strategy. We know we are worth so much more in Whose we are than who we could ever be on our own in this world, or through our social media account.

There isn't a single accomplishment, a single success, or a single award the world can give that will make you feel as known as you are by your Father in Heaven.

Let's close this out in prayer, friend.

Lord,

Thank You for creating something within me that is bigger than myself. Thank You for how You deeply care for me enough to discipline me so I can rise up to your standards and not conform to the standards of this world. Thank You for loving me even when I felt I was hard to love. Thank You for the opportunity you have given me to become more for Your glory and not my own. Thank You for the ability I have to gather in community with others who are created differently than I am so we can shine Your light brighter and wider into every dark crevice in this world to let You be known.

Correct me. Mold me. Take me through the fire so I can be refined into the warrior you need in the spiritual battles that will arise.

Allow me to extend the same love and mercy towards others that you extend to me.

You are such a wonderful Father and I am thankful for the way You intricately designed me so that I can uniquely show others Your glory and Your love.

I am so thankful to be deeply known by You.

Amen.

You

Are

Known.

Connect with Shelbey!

Facebook: Shelbey Faye Kendall

Instagram: @shelbeykendall

ABOUT THE AUTHOR

Hey friend! I'm Shelbey. I'm a wife, momma, dreamer, entrepreneur and most of all—daughter of Christ. If we were sitting across the table at a local coffee shop with iced vanilla lattes in hand, I would skip the small talk. I've always been awkward with talking about the weather. I'm okay with sitting quietly until something of deeper meaning bubbles up. I wear my heart on my sleeve. I love to go for runs with the newest Christian playlist blasting loudly in my headphones. My love language is gifts and words of affirmation. I love bright colors and flowers. Open skies and sunsets fill my soul. I'm an Enneagram 2, wing 3 and my color personality is a Yellow/Red. I love writing and believe I was called to write to encourage and help others on their own unique journeys. I believe the best in others and I believe the best in you. May you and I both be on a journey of growth in Whose we are. I can't wait to experience His Kingdom rising up with all the uniqueness He has beautifully given within all of us.

Made in the USA
Columbia, SC
09 May 2019